WINNING WITH SHARES

Also by Alvin Hall

MONEY FOR LIFE

WINNING WITH SHARES

Investing wisely and profitably in the stock market

Alvin Hall

with Philip Coggan

Hodder & Stoughton

6 8 10 9 7

A CIP catalogue record for this title is available from the British Library

ISBN 0 340 79338 4

Typeset in Palatino by Palimpsest Book Production Limited,
Polmont, Stirlingshire
Printed and bound in Great Britain by
Clays Ltd, St Ives plc

Hodder and Stoughton
A division of Hodder Headline
338 Euston Road
London NW1 3BH

DEDICATION

This book is dedicated to the people who attended my work-shops and speeches on investing in the United Kingdom. The challenging questions they asked, as well as the observations, opinions, and personal experiences they shared with me, inspired and helped shape the presentation of the information in this book.

ACKNOWLEDGEMENTS

While writing this book, an old folk saying kept popping up in my mind: if you see me fighting with a bear, you'd better help the bear. As this book developed, I discovered that the topic was indeed somewhat of a bear and that, unlike in the saying, I was the one who needed some help – especially in gaining an in-depth understanding of the terms and practices that are unique to the UK markets, and that are distinctly different from the US markets. This book could not have been written without the knowledge, patience, and generosity of Philip Coggan. His detailed knowledge and experience as financial news editor and writer combined with my skills as a guilelessly questioning 'outsider' resulted, we hope, in a book that inexperienced and experienced investors will find informative and useful when making investment decisions.

Other friends and colleagues also helped me to make the information in this book easy to read, more clear, and always focused 'on the money.' Alex Prud'homme and Karl Weber, as always, provided invaluable assistance in helping me to put my voice and personal experiences in the book. Belinda Gregg, Mike Hall, and Nigel Johnson-Hill provided their honest and frank criticism, which enabled me not only to improve this book but also to see how I can continue to make it better with each new edition.

Rowena Webb, Emma Heyworth-Dunn and many people at Hodder and Stoughton deserve a special thanks for their patience in giving me the additional time I needed to change, amend, edit, and refine this book. Thanks to Vicki McIvor, my agent, for her encouragement and kind words. And finally, thanks to my friends in the UK who willingly talk about the stocks they buy, the good and bad investments they have made, and their ideas about how stocks, unit trusts, and investment trusts make – or lose – money for them. Our talks helped me to understand the myths and misconceptions that many people have about investing in stocks. I have tried to use them to fill this book with the facts we all need to know in order to invest wisely and profitably.

CONTENTS

DISCIPLINE, PATIENCE . . . AND A LITTLE LUCK

I**N December 1982, shortly after I began working in the financial business, one of the grand old men of Wall Street took me aside, and in a rather bemused voice, said: 'You know what's strange about this business, Alvin? It seems that practically every person you meet wants to invest in shares, yet very few of them bother to learn how the market actually works. It never ceases to amaze me how many people are willing to throw their money away on half-baked tips or ridiculous get-rich-quick schemes. Inevitably, they learn about investing the hard way, by losing lots of money. But the truth is you don't have to be a genius to succeed in the stock market. To make money with shares you need *discipline* and *patience* – and a little *luck*.'

I have never forgotten his words. They inspired me to educate myself on how financial markets work, provided me with the foundation to make many of my most successful investments, and ultimately became the genesis of this book.

Winning with Shares is designed to help you make intelligent and profitable investments in the stock market. The information in these pages is drawn from: (1) the nearly twenty years I have spent teaching this subject to laymen and financial professionals; (2) my own good and bad experiences as an investor; (3) the many discussions with friends and professional investors I've had on the subject; (4) the fact that making money can be fun – even thrilling – and occasionally enlightening; (5) my sincere belief that with *discipline, patience*, and an understanding of your *risk tolerance* any of us can learn to make informed choices about our investments, and, with a little *luck*, can thereby provide ourselves with a comfortable financial future.

My first book in the UK, *Money for Life*, was a general primer on personal finance. *Winning with Shares* is a different kind of book: it's focused solely on explaining how to invest in the stock market. I wrote this book because I have never forgotten how I felt as a beginning investor: uncertain, sceptical, excited, terrified, and a bit confused about what it meant to put my hard-earned money into an abstract thing called shares.

There is, however, no reward without risk. When you own shares you have a stake in a business: if that business prospers, your money will grow along with it; if the enterprise struggles, your investment will wilt. You might not be lucky enough to pick the next Microsoft or Vodafone, but provided you choose well-managed companies in good businesses, and you wait patiently for your returns, you can do far better in the stock market than you would if you stuck all your money in a building society.

Indeed, of all the ways people have historically built wealth – through savings, buying real estate, investing in gilts – one method has always provided superior returns: the stock market. Here are some statistics, courtesy of Barclays Capital, illustrating this fact on a before-tax basis. If you had deposited £1,000 in a building society in 1945, it would have been worth

£52,887 at the end of 1999. That same £1,000 invested in gilts would have grown to only £30,180. However, if you had invested the same amount in the stock market and reinvested all the dividends, it would have been worth £1,031,200. Even considering inflation, that's not a bad return. As we say in America, case closed.

On my first foray into share ownership, I did exactly what the grand old financier had warned me *not* to do. Acting on a 'great tip' from a well-connected friend of a friend (his last name was the same as one of the most prestigious brokerage firms in the US), I invested fully 25 per cent of my savings in a 'hot stock' – US Healthcare – that I knew nothing about. The result? US Healthcare's share price plummeted the week after I bought it, and never recovered while I held it. Even prayer did not lift it from its oh so lowly depths. I was one of the lemmings who learned about investing the hard way. After selling off my investment at a substantial loss, I cursed my bad luck, my friend's friend, fate, and even the 'stupid' market – but mostly I cursed myself. After all, who decided to throw a quarter of his savings away on a half-baked tip about a company he know nothing about? I berated the face in the mirror for being a fool.

Once I'd worked the frustration out of my system (without the help of a therapist), I decided not to let my beginner's mistake scare me away from learning how to invest. I applied myself to the task: I read books, magazines and newspapers on investing, I watched how and where others invested, I asked everyone I knew question after question about how *they* invested, and I continued to put small amounts of my money into well-researched shares.

Working this way, I made two big breakthroughs: I decided on *what kind of shares* I would invest in, and I settled on an *investing style* that suited my personality, my ability to tolerate a certain level of financial risk, and my financial profile. These are important decisions for you to make, as well, and perhaps my experience will be instructive.

Recognising that I would never know everything about every share listed on the Stock Exchange, I decided to focus my research on the kinds of companies that fascinated me. I am personally interested in high-tech products and companies that will affect all our futures, so I chose to invest in those businesses that I could understand. Narrowing down the kind of investments I would make was a huge relief. Now I was actually interested in my investments, and could speak knowledgeably about them (or at least pretend to). When personal computers began to make headlines, for example, I bought Dell Computer shares. When the Internet began to gain momentum, I invested in Cisco Systems. As the biotechnology industry began to show promise, I chose to put my money in biotech leaders such as Amgen and Genentech. I did well with these investments, many of which I still own, while continuing to refine my investment technique. And yes, I did pick some losers – stocks that made me lose both sleep and money. But I learned to cut my losses as soon as I realised my mistake. And after what I call my 'cool-down period', which could last weeks or months depending on the financial – and emotional – damage, I began looking for the next investment opportunity with more experience and wisdom.

Thanks to my US Healthcare débâcle, I had already learned that I would never make it as a 'trend spotter' – one of those lucky speculators who can foresee an emerging investment trend and make a financial killing overnight. Rather, I concentrated on investing in market leaders, and chose shares with long-term growth and value prospects over short-term gain. Picking such investments requires a great deal of patience and discipline, not to mention a bit of luck.

My initial plan was to build up a position of at least 100 shares in every company I invested in. In the UK an equivalent approach would be to put at least £1,000 into each company. But because I wasn't earning much money, I had to acquire my shares in a step-by-step way. I'd buy whatever I could afford – ten, fifteen or thirty shares at a time – but always with the intention of holding on to the investment for a minimum of five years. In the late 1980s, for example, I began to acquire shares in Intel, the computer chip maker, a few shares at a time. It took me about a year to reach my goal of 100 Intel shares, but now I'm very glad that I made the necessary effort. I haven't sold many of my Intel shares, and in the last decade their value has grown exponentially. Today, even after a steep drop in the price of the shares, that investment and others allow me to feel secure in the knowledge that I have built up a comfortable financial cushion. But I must honestly admit that a severe market drop can still make me a little nervous and I do have to stop myself from checking stock prices on a daily basis when this happens.

Investing in the stock market was a big step for me, but through trial and error I've come to understand and enjoy it – and I've even managed to earn some respectable returns along the way. This is something you can learn to do, too, and I've written this book to help demystify the process.

Winning with Shares does not assume that you know anything about the stock market. In fact, it assumes that you know little to nothing about it, but are willing to learn – and that you are willing to *work* at it. And it will take some work.

Let's be honest: the subject of shares can be dry at times, and some of the terms used to describe the stock market can be dauntingly technical. The language can sometimes be confusing. For example, shares are also known as equities. And you will often see the term stocks and shares used interchangeably. Shares are traded on the *stock market*. In the US we call ordinary shares common stock.

But don't let that turn you off. There is a reason for it: financial jargon has evolved over hundreds of years to describe a very specific set of ideas, procedures and products. Many of these phrases – such as 'price-earnings ratio', 'dividend cover', or 'technical analysis' – simply cannot be made warm and fuzzy. There is no easy, user-friendly substitute for them. And rather than dumbing-down any of the information here (which won't benefit you), I've provided definitions throughout the text and in the Glossary.

If you really want to win with shares, you'll need to learn what these financial terms mean and how they are used in the industry. You will also have to spend time thinking about the ideas behind them. In short, you must invest your *time* before you invest your *money*.

My interest in the UK stock market goes back to the mid-1980s, when I first came to London, and heard people in the City referring to 'stocks and shares'. This phrase baffled me: in the US, the words 'stock' and 'share' are used interchangeably. When I asked about the phrase, Londoners told me they used the phrase because that is what they had always said. When I pushed further, they added that they wouldn't dare ask a City professional what the difference between a stock and a share is because it would reveal how little they knew.

I am not so deferential. Eventually, I discovered that in the UK the term 'stocks' was historically used to refer to bonds (debt securities that pay interest) and the term 'shares' was used to refer to ordinary and preferred shares (those securities representing ownership in the company and paying dividends). So saying 'stocks and shares' is the equivalent of saying 'bonds and shares'.

While this distinction is rarely made by professionals, many novice investors continue to parrot the phrase, never questioning what it really means. This struck me as an interesting cultural difference. At first, the polite unwillingness of the average person in Britain to get clear explanations about his or her *own money* struck me as irresponsible – like abdicating one's financial decisions to that special someone with whom you only speak the 'international language of love'. Well, we all know the result of that: trouble! Now, after talking about money with Britons for years, I understand the psychology better. Most new investors would like to educate themselves in private, at their own pace; they want clear and practical answers, without embarrassment. They want to digest what they learn, and to use the information as they need it.

In the meantime, I began to wonder in what other ways the UK stock market differs from its American counterpart. What types of companies interest the typical British investor? Who *is* the typical British investor, and how does he or she regard the markets: as a place for gamblers and speculators, as a secret society open only to those with connections and sophisticated financial skills, or as a place where even common folk could build wealth over time? How do these investors use the markets to make money? How easy is it to do the necessary research? What kinds of information are public companies required to disclose to shareholders, when were they required to disclose it, and how can I find it? These are just a few of the questions I have asked, and been asked, over the years, and I have addressed them in this book.

Winning with Shares is designed as an easy-to-use guide to understanding the stock market and investing in shares. One way to think of it is as a peek inside the City's walls, a place where some professionals would rather you didn't tread. What you'll discover is that once you understand a few basic principles, it really doesn't take a genius to succeed in the stock market.

I encourage you to use this book as you see fit: read it straight through from beginning to end, skip from chapter to chapter, or dip into a section here and there. It's designed to be easy for you to review what you've learned and to build on that knowledge as you gain confidence and experience.

There is no undisclosed City secret to making a good investment and there is not one method that is perfect for everyone. To invest successfully there must be a willingness on your part to gain some knowledge of the industry and the business in which are thinking about investing your money. It takes an awareness of your own risk tolerance, discipline and patience. And again, it takes a bit of luck. I hope this book helps you to understand how you can use the stock market as part of your overall financial strategy to build your own comfortable financial future.

CHAPTER ONE

YOUR INVESTMENT PSYCHOLOGY: IS INVESTING IN STOCKS FOR YOU?

I T'S a basic human desire to want comfort, but everyone's needs and desires are different. For me, comfort means having enough income to buy an apartment with a terrace in a nice doorman building, to contribute the maximum amount each year to my retirement plan, to build a small but excellent art collection, and to be able to upgrade myself to business class when I fly. For you it might mean having a large house with a beautiful and spacious garden, taking luxurious holidays, or having a second home in Spain or the south of France. And life is even better when there's money left over after you've given yourself a few *extra* comforts.

Today, in order for many of us to achieve our desired level of comfort, we'll need to make part of the money we put away grow faster than it would if we simply deposited it in a building society. The facts I quoted in the Introduction show that investing in the stock market has historically been the best way to achieve this financial growth. But investing in shares is not something to be undertaken lightly. Share owner-ship has potentially great advantages, but it is *always* a risky proposition. Therefore you must ask yourself: 'Is this type of investing the right thing for me?'

If you have no savings and/or lots of credit card debt, then I highly recommend you get those personal finances sorted before you even think about investing money in the stock market. If you are a nervous worrier or a person who dislikes risk, you are probably not psychologically suited to share ownership, or you may be suited to a very limited approach. If you are a cautious person, you may be happy with a lower return from the stock market (yet one that is better than a building society) in exchange for limited risk. Owning shares requires patience and the ability not to become over-confident when the market goes up or panic if the value of your investment falls, say, 5, 10, or even 20 per cent in a single day.

I suspect that, since you've gone to the trouble of reading this book, you intend to take a stab at owning shares. But before you take the plunge, try answering the following questions about money and your investment goals – and answer them honestly! Your answers will help you determine what kind of money personality you have and consequently enable you to craft an investment strategy that best suits your temperament, skills and financial situation.

ARE YOU WILLING TO RISK YOUR MONEY?

- Do you only focus optimistically on the potential gains from an investment, completely ignoring or denying the possibility of loss?
- If you buy a stock and the price rises do you focus on the gains you've made or the gains you would lose if the price declined?
- How would you feel if you buy shares and the next day their market price 'tanked' – as they say in the City?

If you have ever lost money, has that loss become the first thing that you remember when someone mentions an 'investment' opportunity?

There is no way to invest in the stock market without placing your money at risk. I am sometimes asked during my speeches if I know of a safe stock – i.e., one with little or no risk – and a high return. If such a share were available in the market, you can be sure that every institution would rush out and buy it before you or I could.

Risk and reward always go hand in hand. The more risk you take in share ownership, the greater your potential rewards – and losses. Figuring out if you can tolerate having your money at risk is a tricky calculation, part involving numbers (i.e., the amount of money you are willing to risk) and part involving your emotions. While it's easy to be seduced by tales of huge, 'easy' wins on the stock market, the risk of losing money is very real. I know a few people who have done well through investing in shares, and I know people who have been undone by their investing habits. The key element in the two stories that follow is not whether these people were willing to risk their money, but the way in which they were willing to risk it.

A lady I know in her mid-thirties decided that she was unhappy with the return she and husband were getting by playing it completely safe. She decided to take responsibility for making investment decisions for her and her husband's retirement. She was only interested in what's known as bellwether stocks – those companies that are the leaders of their business sectors and are often used to determine the health and future prospects of that sector. Her motto was 'I only want to own the best.' And she wisely limited the number of sectors that she would hold shares in at any given time. As soon as one of these stocks started to 'fall out of bed' – i.e., their long-term growth prospects dimmed and the price began to decline – she would sell it, capture her profits, and begin looking for another sector. She never felt the need to jump right back into the market. While she will not be, to use her own words, 'the richest grave in the cemetery', her retirement will be 'comfortable enough to make me happy'. This lady's focus, diligence and thoughtful tolerance of risk helped her to gain the insight she needed to build successfully a nice retirement for herself and her husband.

How different her story is to another, older friend who kept talking about investing in stocks but never did anything because he was, shall we say, a little out of touch with his own nervousness about losing money. However, when he got some money from a redundancy package he became emboldened. He called me up and asked me about some stocks that had been tipped in newspapers and magazines. His belief was that if he spread this money around lots of these penny stocks, eventually one of them would pay off. Well, guess what? None of them paid off. He couldn't believe it. Disillusioned and angry, he's still holding the stocks, waiting and hoping and wishing and praying to 'just make back the money I put in' as more and more of them go lower and lower. I suspect he'll be holding them until God calls him – or those companies – home.

The market can fall more than 20 per cent in a day, (as it did in 1987) or over a short period (as it did in the third and fourth quarters of 2000), and individual shares can become worthless virtually overnight if the company goes bankrupt. Even without witnessing those extremes, share prices *are* volatile. If the risk of losing 10 per cent in one day is unacceptable and unimaginable to you, then perhaps you should try putting your money into a more sedate and safe vehicle, such as a building society account or National Savings.

In reality most people can tolerate having some of their money at risk, usually if the risk is very low. Take real estate, for example. The value of your property does not go up in a straight line. During certain economic periods the value can decline. However, your home is a tangible asset that you can enjoy even when its value is decreasing. Stocks are intangible, providing little creature comfort and certainly no emotional comfort when prices are down. In the light of this comparison, perhaps the question that introduced this section should be: 'On what are you willing to risk your money?'

How much can you afford to invest?

If you decide you *can* bear the risk associated with investing in stocks and that you are patient enough to invest for the long term, then you should consider whether you can really afford to put money into shares. The golden rule of investing is: 'Don't ever put money in the stock market that you can't afford to lose.' However, it is not quite that simple. You need to look at your total financial situation – called your financial profile – before you can know that you have the money to invest.

Have you set up and are contributing regularly to a pension scheme? Do you have all your basic insurance needs covered? Have you got enough 'rainy day' money saved for such exigencies as a major car or home repair, or being laid off unexpectedly, or temporarily disabled? Once all the basics are covered then it is probably a prudent idea to invest some of your *extra* income or savings directly in shares or in a unit trust. Let's call this extra money your 'investable funds'.

The process of determining how much of this money should be invested in stocks and other types of securities is known as asset allocation. There are many models or formulae that suggest how much of your investable funds should be invested in stocks. A good way to begin is to look at investing in stocks in a strategic way. Ask yourself: 'What kind of return is reasonable to expect given the risk I am willing to take?' The answer to this question will help you focus on the types of shares classified by their risk (see Chapter 2) you want to buy.

I know it sounds backwards to start this way. But the benefit of this approach is that you focus on the end result and how to get there, as opposed to looking at every share you purchase as your next 'moonshot' to riches. If, for example, you are willing to accept a return that is less than the stock market's overall return (but better than that of a building society) in exchange for lower risk to the money you've invested, then your money should be in more conservative stocks. If you are willing to accept a return that is in line with the overall market as measured by a specific index like the FTSE 100, then buy a tracker fund. These are the easiest decisions. However, if you want a return that is better than the market, then you have to put together a combination of high-, medium-, and low-risk shares or unit trusts that is likely to provide this return.

In summary, think of your investable funds as that portion of your overall assets that you can place at risk, always keeping in mind your expectation of return, in hopes of making your money work harder for you, but whose loss will not diminish your lifestyle.

How patient are you?

Patience and discipline are the watchwords for good investing. For a typical investor – whether beginning or with moderate experience – it is inappropriate to buy shares looking for a quick return to pay for your next summer holiday. If your goal as a beginning investor is to make money fast, the stock market isn't the place for you. Frankly, you'd probably be better off gambling at the racetrack.

Successful investing takes time. It's possible, of course, to achieve an impressive return with a portfolio of shares that you have held for a year or two. But the odds work best in your favour if you can keep your money in shares for at least five years.

My own rule of thumb is to look for companies in my area of interest whose growth prospects, especially earnings growth, are predicted by a majority of the analysts who follow the stock to be strong during a five-year period. I readily admit that I'm a little too much of a coward to buy shares, such as many of the dot coms, that are expected at best to lose less and less money over the next three to five years. That's way beyond my risk tolerance and my patience.

Part of being patient is having the ability to manage your own emotions. During an inevitable market decline, of course the temptation will be to check the prices every hour. This just increases your level of anxiety and may cause you to make an irrational decision. On the other hand you also need to be patient when the price of a stock is rising. Don't be too quick to take your profits. I have heard many, many people rationalise selling securities to capture their profits saying that they don't want to be too greedy. A more rational approach would be to research whether the company's growth prospects are still strong, and if so its share price should continue to increase.

ARE YOU TOO BUSY TO FOLLOW THE MARKETS REGULARLY?

Keeping track of your investments doesn't have to be a full-time job. Many new investors have this idea that people who invest in stocks are obsessed by the market, that it is all they think about twenty-four hours a day! Personally, I do not check the prices of my stocks every day. In fact, I only check the prices on Sunday, when the information I find out may necessitate my falling on my knees in prayer! Also, because it is the weekend, I have some time to think instead of just reacting rashly. By setting a fixed and limited amount of time that I will devote to reviewing the performance of my holdings, I don't feel as if it has taken over my life or is a burden. In fact it usually takes less time than reviewing and balancing my current account.

I use the same approach to look for new investment ideas. When I first started to invest, I used to believe that when I sold some shares I had to reinvest the money immediately in others. This urgency led me, regrettably, to make some poorly researched investments. Now I take my time. I am happy holding my profits in cash, earning modest interest, until I can find and research the next company's shares in which I will invest. It does take a bit of time to research interesting companies with good growth prospects.

If your job and/or family life leave no time for this kind of research, you may want to invest in a unit or investment trust (where a professional manager makes all the decisions) or work closely with a broker who will provide you with ideas and the printed research for you to evaluate. The key thing is to figure out a method of following the performance of your investments that not only keeps you informed, but also makes it interesting and fun.

ARE YOU INTERESTED IN FINANCE?

Many people will read this question and immediately interpret it to mean: 'Are you interested in economics?' That's not what I mean. I want you to ask yourself if you are interested in how money works. How does Tesco's make a profit? What caused the venerable Marks & Spencer's sales to decline? How does your bank make the majority of its profits? Who makes money from your credit card transactions? If you wonder about these sorts of things, then you are interested in finance. And you can build on this nascent interest to develop your interest in a particular business sector, which could in turn lead to your purchasing shares. You most certainly don't have to be an economist or an accountant to be able to evaluate an investment. But you do need some level of curiosity.

DO YOU HAVE A FIELD OF EXPERTISE?

This question comes out of the previous one about your interest in finance. What about your interest in other business areas? Do you have an observation, an insight based on experience, or some kind of specialised knowledge that might give you a keener insight about a particular sector of the stock market? Are you, for example, a doctor who has found an incredibly helpful new medical device, a computer nerd who has spotted a new software or an emerging trend in that industry, or a dedicated shopper aware of a new product that everyone is buying? These are ripe opportunities that you can explore and perhaps invest in, sometimes before the trend lemmings catch on!

My favourite story involves a friend of mine who for years ran a good, but struggling word-processing firm. He worked very hard, but always seemed to lack the ability to organise his business. One day when he was doing some work for me, I told him that I was about to buy a new computer and asked if he had any recommendations. He told me which brand he liked (primarily because it was cheap), but said that most of the firms he was doing work for were ordering another brand that was a little more expensive. This added cost, he noted, was offset by the product's reliability and the company's excellent customer service. I asked him if he owned any shares in the computer maker. He looked at me quizzically and said, 'I never thought about that.' The investment that was right under his nose would eventually make him a good deal of money over a five-year period.

Recently, when he was preparing a Powerpoint presentation for me, I asked about his shares. He noted that his clients were ordering new computers at a slower pace and that the focus seemed to be shifting. 'I think it is time to sell. The pace of the company's growth must be slowing if my clients are ordering less.' Less than six months later the company issued an earnings warning. Indeed both its sales and earnings would be lower than expected.

The old adage that sometimes a simple idea is the best idea comes to mind when I think about my friend's investment. Just by looking at what is going on in your daily profession or life may plant the seed of a great investment idea. While you are already ahead because you have an interest or connection to the company or its core business, you still need to do your research. Keep in mind that a good product is not everything. There are many other factors to consider before putting your money into a company. That new wonder drug you've heard about could represent only a tiny percentage of a company's sales. Or the drug might be great, but the business might be poorly managed. And even a good business might not be worth buying if investors have already pushed the share price too high. This is where the discipline of focused research comes into play.

Thinking this way might give you a good place to start when it comes to researching what sort of shares you'd like to invest in. Opportunity is literally all around you. This type of 'market research' is really an advanced form of common sense; it's a way to forecast future success before others do by paying attention to the world around you.

WHY ARE YOU INVESTING?

'To make money' is the usual answer to this question. And it is an inadequate response. There are many other ways to make money in the world than the stock market, and many of these are less risky. Before you invest your first pound in a share, you must know the reasons why you are taking this step.

- Are you investing because it's currently a fad?
- Are you investing because you saw all the dot.comers making money and you want some of the action?
- Did someone 'in the know' give you a tip and you are taking advantage of the information?
- Do you see the stock market as a supplemental way to help your money grow faster for you?
- Are you looking to make your retirement savings grow faster over a long period of time than they would in a building society?
- Are you curious about shares and have always wanted to learn about how they work?
- Are you looking to get rich quick?

To be a good investor and to give yourself a reasonable chance of achieving your goal, you must clearly know why you are investing. My own primary investment goal, for example, has always been to accumulate money for a comfortable, travel-filled retirement. It has never been my objective to retire at forty-five and live off the money I've invested. (Frankly, I think I enjoy working a little too much.) A secondary objective was always to make stock picking fun and educational. But all of us need to be aware of our limitations. You must allow yourself room to learn and grow. My own strategy evolved over time as I learned and grew as an investor.

When people learn that I come from a very poor background, many assume that I have been willing to take huge investment risks in order to get ahead. But this is overly simplistic. In fact, my investing technique evolved slowly, from super-conservative to mildly risk-taking. In the early years I invested solely in blue-chip shares: GE, Glaxo-Wellcome (now GlaxoSmithKline), IBM, Johnson & Johnson, British Telecom. As I gained confidence in my abilities, I came to believe that my early investments were too conservative for my age and needs. So I carefully planned how I'd move up to the next tier of risk.

Today, on a risk scale of 1 to 10, I rate myself around 7, depending on how full the moon is. Or, to put it another way: while I'm not trendy enough to buy shares in risky dot.coms, I have put my hard-earned money into some of the companies that make the Internet run. Looking forward I can see the impact of these companies' products on my own and others' lives and finances.

You have to decide what the right amount of risk is for you. Like me, you might not be lucky the first time you purchase a share. But if you are prepared to put in some effort, then it is possible to find good companies. And once you get the stock market bug, you will find it is an exciting, intellectually challenging and profitable pursuit. Just think – you are pitting your brains against some of the most savvy people on the planet. Good luck and keep it fun!

CHAPTER TWO

THE TYPES OF SHARES
AND HOW THEY WORK

W HAT is a share? Technically speaking, a share is a security representing part-ownership of a company and entitling its owner to the right to receive dividends (a portion of the company's earnings distributed to shareholders). In plain language, a share is just what it says it is: a share of the ownership and assets of a company.

The market price of a share rises and falls along with the fortunes of the company. A share is quite different from a gilt, or bond, which is a loan. You are a creditor of the issuer when you buy a bond and are entitled to receive a fixed rate of interest for the term of the loan. As a shareowner, however, you will have a much greater chance for profit (and loss), and a quite different set of rights compared to those of a creditor. Once shares are issued, they have an indefinite life: they can trade in the market for ever. So if you want to sell your shares in a company you can't simply ring up its founder and ask for your money back. You'll have to call a stockbroker, who will try to find another investor to buy them from you. Most companies have a large number of shares trading in the market and many shareholders. This makes selling and purchasing the shares relatively easy and quick.

This is quite a different type of investment from putting your money into a bank savings account or a building society. There are no guarantees that you will profit from shares, but there are no restrictions on your earning potential, especially from the price appreciation of the stock. If you go through life putting all your money in the Halifax you will never be poor, but nor will you accumulate a large amount of money that could improve significantly your standard of living. By investing in shares you at least give yourself the chance to watch your money grow more quickly and the potential to make a material change in your lifestyle. You are also placing your money at greater risk.

By far the most frequently issued share in the UK is the *ordinary share*. It gives investors a share in the growth of the company, the right to vote on important company decisions, and the right to receive dividends (a payment that some companies distribute to shareholders, usually twice but sometimes four times a year). Despite its name, there is nothing ordinary about the ordinary share's potential for growth.

If you pick the right share and hold on to it long enough, you could become wealthy. One thousand pounds invested in Sage, a software company, at the start of the 1990s, for example, turned into £281,000 by the year 2000.

Shares came into existence as a way to enable companies to raise capital (money) by selling a portion of the ownership in the business in exchange for money. Imagine a business owned by a few partners. If it went bust the creditors could pursue the partners for every last penny. The business owners could lose their homes, their jewellery, even the clothes they stood up in. But shares have the advantage of limited liability. When you invest money in shares, you know that the most you can lose is the amount you put in. If the company goes bust, the creditors cannot touch you. Without this principle in place, a lot of businesses would never be funded and the economy would be a lot smaller than it is today.

When a company is set up, someone has to own it. Often it will be just one person. But many companies are started by a group of people, and as they grow more people are likely to get involved. Obviously there has to be some agreement about how the profits of the business will be distributed; and if the company is sold, how the proceeds will be carved up. Otherwise there will be enormous arguments. So the founders will make some decision: Fred put up the money, so he gets 60 per cent; Sue had the idea, so she gets 30 per cent, and so on.

When you look at a share certificate, you may see that it says something like Acme Company's 25p share or 50p share. It is easy to get confused by this. Don't think that it means your shares are worth just 25p or 50p. This is what is known as the *par value* of the share. Except in very limited circumstances (when the company is in trouble), it has no meaning at all. For legal reasons, all shares have to have a par value – it could be 1p or 50p or £1 – but the price they trade at in the market can reach into the hundreds or thousands of pounds.

Most small businesses stay small, but a few grow rapidly. As they do, they need more money to invest in new factories or technologies, buy more supplies, or promote and market their products. They can borrow some of that money from banks, but the interest on bank loans (especially for risky small businesses) can be prohibitively expensive. So many companies look to outside investors who are willing to buy equity, or part-ownership, in the business. In some cases, these may be friends or family members. One friend of Anita

Roddick, for example, put up £10,000 to help her build Body Shop, and ended up a multi-millionaire.

Small companies can also turn to specialist investors called *venture capitalists* (VCs) who invest in risky projects in the hope that they will see high rewards. Venture capitalists recognise that eight or nine out of ten companies they invest in will fail, but count on recouping those losses – and making a tidy profit – from the one or two winners they pick.

The process of involving outsiders involves good news and bad news for company founders. The good news is that they get capital to expand their business without paying high rates of interest; the bad news is that they trade some of their own equity (ownership) in return. This trade-off sometimes leads to tension, and it is not unheard of for outside investors to take control of a company they feel is not being managed well. On the other hand, without investors' money, businesses find it difficult to grow.

Imagine a company called Hall Fashions, which sells men's suits. There are 100 shares in issue and Arthur and his sister Aretha own fifty each. They would like to open a new store in the West End of London, but that is an expensive proposition. So they go along to Speculators Limited, a venture capital group that agrees to put up the money in return for fifty new shares. Arthur and Aretha can now open their new store. But while they used each to own half the business, now they each just own a third. Now they have to listen to an outsider's view about how they should run their company. What Arthur and Aretha hope, of course, is that they end up with a smaller share of a much bigger pie.

Eventually, some businesses grow too big to be supported by just one or two outside investors. They need to attract funds from the wider investor community, from pension funds and insurance companies, and from individuals like you and me. That is when they decide to 'float' (issue shares) on the stock market.

This doesn't happen as often as you might think. There are hundreds of thousands of businesses in the UK but only around 2,500 of them are quoted on the stock market. They range from minnows, worth less than £1 million, to whales like Vodafone that are worth tens of billions of pounds. This spectrum gives investors like you a big choice of companies to invest in.

ORDINARY SHAREHOLDERS' RIGHTS

As an investor, it's important that you keep a wary eye on the company's management, to make sure that they are acting in the interest of shareholders and not feathering their own nest. It is in the interest of directors to make their companies as large as possible, for example – a big company justifies a big salary. And opportunities for companies to build themselves up abound. Bankers ring up company directors every day, urging them to buy a competitor or two. The impression these bankers often like to give is that if companies don't make deals they are wimpy or narrow-minded. Of course, growing through such purchases may be a wise decision that will benefit the investors. But maybe not. Fortunately there are safeguards to protect your investment.

RIGHT TO VOTE

Ordinary shares give the owner a number of important rights. The first is the right to vote on significant issues, such as the approval of new acquisitions or the appointment of directors to the board. Most important of all, companies cannot be taken over without the agreement of the majority of shareholders.

When a vote is due, the company will send them a form,

like an election ballot slip, which allows them to indicate their views. Investors can vote in one of two ways. They can either appoint someone (usually the chairman) who will act as a *proxy* for them. That proxy will then cast votes on the investor's behalf. The other method is for investors to attend the company's meetings and vote for themselves.

There are two types of company meetings, the *annual general meeting* (AGM) and the *extraordinary general meeting* (EGM). AGMs, as the name suggests, are held every year; EGMs occur when the company needs to do something special, like ratify a big acquisition. While they are often dull affairs – held somewhere close to the company's headquarters, which can involve a long journey – some AGMs and EGMs are interesting. For a start, some companies supply food and drink to reward their loyal shareholders. Others can be controversial: protesters have dogged companies such as Hanson (over mining in a Native American burial site) and BAE Systems (over arms exports to Indonesia). And the meetings do give you the chance to see and question the executives who run the company you've put your money into. At the very least, attending such a meeting puts a human face on your investment, and allows you to judge more clearly whether the company is being run in the interests of shareholders.

DIVIDENDS

All shareholders have the right to receive dividends. When paid, these come from a portion of a company's profits remaining after it has paid all operations expenses, interest on any outstanding debt and taxes. Not all companies pay dividends, but most UK companies do, usually twice or four times a year. All dividends must be declared by the company's board of directors.

Dividend payments vary substantially among companies.

Some deliberately do not pay a dividend at all; they reinvest all their profits back into the business. Others pay only a small dividend, again on the principle that they need to hold on to all their cash. Both cases are typical of young growth companies in new business areas. Investors in these types of companies hope to make money on the stocks from their capital growth – i.e., the increase in market price of the shares.

Some companies, usually those in mature or slow-growth industries, such as utilities, have few exciting investment opportunities. There is not likely to be any significant increase in either sales or market share, and therefore no substantial increase in the market price of the companies' shares. In such circumstances, these companies pay out the bulk of their profits in the form of dividends to shareholders. In doing so, they make themselves attractive to investors who are interested in a steady, predictable stream of income instead of capital gains.

The dividend payments that you receive when you first begin investing may not seem like much, at first. But they can grow over time, sometimes significantly, as companies' boards of directors periodically choose to increase the amount of the pay-out. If you buy a share in your forties, say, you could find it pays a very nice dividend indeed by the time you are ready to retire. This is particularly true if you don't need the income right now and choose to take advantage of two schemes that some companies offer: (1) a dividend reinvestment plan (the ability to reinvest dividends automatically in the companies' shares); (2) the ability to take extra shares instead of cash. (This is known as a scrip offering.) Both methods are good ways of increasing the growth of the money you are investing over the long term. (To find out more about dividend reinvestment or scrip offering contact the company in which you own shares.)

This increased growth is all due to a marvel known as *compounding*. Suppose you have 100 shares, each worth £1, and the company pays a dividend of 2p a share. That will give you a payment of £2, which you use to buy two more shares. Next year, the company pays a dividend of 2.1p a share. You now receive the dividend on 102 shares. So your dividend is now £2.14, which you reinvest to buy more shares. And so on. Year after year, the number of shares you own in the company increases, and the amount of the dividend payment you can reinvest also increases. When you retire you may choose to begin receiving the payments as cash (instead of reinvesting them), and you may find you have enough shares to generate a handsome income. Research from Barclays Capital shows that over the past century, two-thirds of the profits from holding shares have come in the form of reinvested dividends.

It is important to keep in mind that both the paying of the dividend and the amount of the payment are at the discretion of a company's board of directors. There is no guarantee of the continual payment of dividends, however. Just as a company can *increase* its dividend payments, it can also *cut* its dividends, or even eliminate the pay-out altogether. This is usually taken as a sign that the company is in trouble, and the firm's share price will usually tumble as a result.

Companies may also issue special dividends from time to time, especially if they have come into a sudden windfall, such as the sale of an unwanted subsidiary. This can be good news, but it is not always as good as it seems. The market price of the share will often fall by the amount of the special dividend because the cash will no longer be working for the good of the business. In a way, all that happens is that shareholders get a bit of their capital back – and then they have to pay tax on it!

Dividends are taxed as normal income, except when they

are held within individual savings accounts (see later in the book).

SPLITS AND BONUSES

When a company senses that its share price is too high (a very subjective decision), it may announce a *bonus*, or *scrip, issue* – that is, it will issue more shares at a reduced price, which is perceived to widen their appeal. Another option, widely used in the US, is a *stock split* – where a company issues more shares to existing shareholders at no additional cost. The effect of this is to lower the price of the shares at issue. So, a one-for-one bonus issue, for example, gives you one extra share for every one you hold, and a two-for-one stock split does the same. Alas, this doesn't mean you've instantly doubled your money, or the percentage of your ownership in the company; the value of the company remains the same. It simply means your ownership is spread over more shares.

Let me explain this principle simply. Supposing you order a pizza from the local takeaway; the pizzeria firm tells you they have a special deal: instead of cutting the pizza into four, they will slice the same size pizza into eight slices. Would you feel that you were getting a better deal? Or look at it another way. You have a £5 note: someone offers a swap for five pound coins. Do you feel any better off?

PRE-EMPTIVE RIGHTS

When it comes to issuing new shares, existing shareholders are protected by *pre-emptive* rights. This ensures that the company cannot issue a substantial amount of new shares without offering its existing shareholders the chance to buy them first.

Why is this important? Say you own 100 shares in Acme Leisure, which has 1,000 shares in total. You own 10 per cent of the company. But the directors of Acme have a close relationship with an outside businessman, Felix Fatcat. They announce they are giving him 250 shares of the company. Suddenly you no longer have 10 per cent of Acme; now your 100 shares represent only 8 per cent of the 1,250 in issue. You have lost influence over the company.

To prevent this injustice, companies have to offer substantial issues of new shares to existing investors in what is known as a *rights issue*. You might be offered one new share for every four you already hold. (The company determines this ratio.) And you are usually offered the new stock at a discount to the current share price.

Let's imagine that Acme is offering one new share for every four you already own. Its shares are currently trading at 100p, and the company offers you each new share at 80p. If you take up your rights, you would now have 125 shares out of the total of 1,250. Thus you would maintain your original 10 per cent holding.

If you didn't have the money available to buy the new shares, you could sell your rights to someone else. The right to buy new shares at 80p when the market price is 100p is obviously worth approximately 20p a share. So you could sell your rights to the 25 shares for about £5. Your percentage holding in the company would have dropped but you would have additional cash as compensation. (Note: The actual formula used to calculate the value of a right is more complicated. This example is designed to show you that you can sell the rights on the stock market for cash.)

INFORMATION

One of the most important rights of shareholders is the right to be informed. The directors must let investors and the overall market know what is going on in the business.

The most important piece of information is the annual report. It gives shareholders an overview of a company's overall status. The annual report should give a full breakdown of the company's profit and loss account, its balance sheet and an explanation of the sources and uses of cash. These figures are prepared by independent auditors who have examined the business. The annual report should also explain what has been happening in each of the company's businesses over the previous year, and provide a breakdown of results by division. This allows investors to see whether the company is 'carrying' any under-performing operations, which perhaps should be sold.

Typical investors can't use the annual report to spot budding corporate fraud. But it does allow you to ask a few questions, such as:

- Is the company's turnover (sales) growing, and if not, why not?
- Are profits boosted by one-off items, such as the sale of a subsidiary?
- Has the level of debt or interest payments risen sharply?
- Are the company's shareholders funds (its net worth) higher than at the end of the previous year?

The 'notes to the accounts' section of a company's annual report can also raise some interesting issues.

- Has the growth in directors' pay outpaced the growth in profits and dividends?
- Have the directors been buying or selling shares? At the very least, asking these questions will give you a better idea of the health of the business and of the calibre of the people who run it.

At the annual general meeting, the chairman should give a statement concerning the level of business in the current year. This can be a very useful guide as to whether the business is going from strength to strength or starting to experience problems.

During the course of the year the company should also announce any significant news to the Stock Exchange. This can come in a host of forms. It may be the winning of a major contract, or a joint venture with another business. It could be news of a takeover. Less encouragingly, it could be a warning that profits will be lower than expected. You'll hear such news on a broadsheet financial report or read it in the business section of your newspaper.

Investors in the company are also required to keep the market informed of their activities, if they are large enough. The Stock Exchange has to be notified when any person or company acquires more than 13 percent of a company's outstanding shares. This can be a useful warning of a pending takeover approach. It also allows investors to see which leading institutions, such as Prudential or Standard Life – two big insurance companies – are big holders of the company's shares, and to spot when those institutions are dumping (selling) the stock.

Directors must also notify the company of any sales or purchases they make of its shares. It's not uncommon for directors to sell. Often, a director's entire net worth will be tied up in a stock, and when there is a sudden need for money – if they buy a new house or get a divorce, say – they will be forced to sell. But if lots of directors are selling their stock in the company at the same time, it could be a bad sign. And if lots of them are buying, that at least shows they believe in the company and are willing to put their money where their mouths are.

Shareholders like you must be fully informed at all times. There should not be a division between a few investors who are 'in the know' and the rest. Such a situation is called 'a false market'. The Stock Exchange strives hard to ensure that false markets are rare and quickly exposed.

LIQUIDATION

What happens to shareholders when a company gives up the ghost? Normally, this is very bad news. Ordinary shareholders come virtually at the bottom of the heap when it comes to getting a pay-out if a company goes into bankruptcy – well after people such as the Inland Revenue and employees owed back pay.

But there can be an exception to this rule. Supposing a company decides to give up its main line of business and sell it to a competitor? The company would suddenly get a whole injection of cash, and shareholders would be entitled to some of that money.

PREFERENCE SHARES

Not everybody wants to take the risks of investing in ordinary shares; after all, there is the risk of losing all your money if the company goes bust. There are more secure ways of investing in companies, chief among which is the *preference share*.

As the name suggests, holders of these shares have preference over ordinary shareholders in two situations: First, dividends must be paid to preference shareholders before they can be paid to ordinary shareholders. And second, if a company goes bankrupt, these shares have preference when the money (if any) is being handed out. In short, preference shareholders have to be paid first, before ordinary shareholders see a penny. Sounds a good deal? Well, it is – but only up to a point.

The preference dividend is fixed. It does not change even as the company makes more money. In contrast, the ordinary dividend can grow. If you invest in a good company, then you will do far better by investing in the ordinary shares than in the preference shares. (Preference shares hold no voting right and no pre-emptive rights.)

Preference shares are often given other features designed to increase their attractiveness to potential shareholders. Three of the most common are discussed below.

Convertible preferred An investment that is a bit more exciting is the *convertible preference* share. This is like a regular preference share, in that it pays a fixed dividend, but it can also be converted into ordinary shares at a set price. Convertible preference shares thus offer investors an each-way bet. It gives them the security of a normal preference share, but if the ordinary share price rises fast enough it also gives investors the chance to reap the benefit.

Cumulative preferred Preference shares can also be *cumulative*. If a company misses a dividend payment on a cumulative preference share, then it will be forced to make up the missed payment in subsequent years. This gives the investors an added layer of security.

Redeemable preferred Another variation is to make preference shares *redeemable*. This means that unlike ordinary shares the preference share will eventually be repaid.

As far as a company is concerned, preference shares are just one more way of raising capital. They are a kind of hybrid between ordinary shares and bonds. They have advantages compared with either: the dividend payment on a preference share will normally be lower than the interest payment on a bond. And the company can issue new preference shares without affecting the percentage of ownership of key and controlling holders.

NEW ISSUES
Many companies have been quoted on the stock market for

a long time; some since the last century. But at one point they all had to come to the market for the first time; when that happens, a company is known as a new issue or an initial public offering (IPO).

Having a public quotation of its share price or value also means that it will be easier for the company to use its shares to acquire other companies. It also means that it will be easier for the company to retain key employees by offering them share options. In both cases, the great advantage of a stock market quotation is that it is much easier for investors to buy and sell the company's shares – a quality that is called *liquidity*. This is because there will always be one or more firms, called *market makers*, who will be willing to deal in the shares. In contrast, if you want to buy or sell shares in an unquoted company, it can be a long and cumbersome process.

Another important reason for a company to join the stock market is to allow its owners to realise some cash. It can be a lot of hard work building up a private company and it is quite common for all the profits to be ploughed back into the business. A stock market quotation may thus give entrepreneurs their first real chance to get their hands on the wealth they have worked so hard to create.

Investors need to keep an eye on the founders. There is nothing wrong with entrepreneurs selling a portion of their stakes to pay off the mortgage, buy a new yacht or whatever. But if the company's founders are selling more than half their holdings, outside investors will undoubtedly be cynical. If the insiders are selling, why should you buy?

Companies normally sell just a limited amount of their shares on flotation; anything from 10 per cent to 30 per cent. Some of the shares may be new and be used to raise money for the business; others may be the shares of the owners or the venture capitalists who backed the company in its early days.

When a company joins the market, it essentially has to sell its merits to the investing public. So it needs an experienced guide to put it in touch with the right investors and to advise it on the price at which it should sell its shares. Those guides are *investment banks* and *stockbrokers*, most of which are based in the City of London.

Both types of company earn a good part of their profits by advising companies and earning fees in the process. New issues are only part of this work; another big area is advising companies on mergers and acquisitions. It is a highly lucrative business: fees on some transactions can run into millions of pounds and investment bankers are some of the best-paid people in the country.

The investment bank or broker will draw up a kind of brochure for a new issue, known as a *prospectus*, which will explain the company's history, its line of business, the names and careers of its management, its profit record over the last few years and its proposed use of the money it is trying to raise. It will also have to explain all the risks involved in backing such a company.

The bank or broker (often both will be involved) will then take the prospectus to the big investors – insurance companies or fund managers. They will find out whether they are willing to buy shares and what price they are prepared to pay.

Pricing the shares is a tricky business. The company obviously wants the maximum possible price. But the investment bank will want the shares to go up in price on the first day of trading, so that the issue is regarded as a success. The happy medium is an issue that goes up 20 to 30 per cent on the first day so that everybody is happy. If the shares double, the new issue investors are delighted but the company's founders may feel they have sold themselves short.

Most new issues in the UK only end up in the pockets of the big institutional investors via what are known as *placings*. Private investors don't get a look-in until the first day of trading when they are normally forced to pay a significantly higher price. This seems unfair, so why does it happen?

The first reason is that the big institutions are very important clients of the banks and brokers, far more important than your John Bulls and Alvin Halls. The banks or brokers want to keep their best clients happy so they give them as many of the shares in the best new issues as possible.

The second reason is that institutional investors have deep pockets. The whole point of coming to the stock market is the ability it gives companies to raise money, not just at the time of the new issue but well into the future. Private investors are unlikely to have the resources to help the company make that big acquisition in a few years' time so many companies prefer to have the big institutions on their side. It is also more costly to deal with private investors; every one has to be sent an annual report, dividend cheque and so on.

The third, and more cynical, reason is that it pays to create a shortage. You know how certain restaurants can be 'hot'. The mere fact that tables are booked up for weeks in advance makes potential customers think the food must be good. That makes them book two months in advance, which makes the restaurant even harder to get into and so on.

The same applies to new issues. If all private investors are excluded from the initial offer, then they will have to buy when trading starts. That will create a big pool of unsatisfied demand for the shares which will mean the price gets forced up, making the company look great and the initial investors very happy.

Luckily, there are some companies that allow private investors in at the new issue level, even if it is only for 20 per cent or so of the shares available. This gives investors a chance to get in on the ground floor. But it is wrong to think that all new issues are automatic money-spinners like most of those privatisation stocks the UK government sold off in the 1980s. In fact, the price of many new issues languish after the flotation.

Having looked at the company's prospectus, it is then up to potential investors to apply for shares by sending in an application form and a cheque to the company's broker.

Even if the issue is a big success, investors can find, as they did with Lastminute.com, that they end up with very few shares each. Applicants for Lastminute shares got just thirty-five shares each, worth £133 at the flotation price. Anyone hoping for instant millions found that their first day profit was just £20, after costs. Just as bad, many investors had sent in cheques for £1,000 or more and had to wait to get the balance of their money back.

Companies that join the stock market have a choice about where they go. Most companies opt for what is called the main market – they get a full listing. This requires them to have a track record of at least three years and for 25 per cent of the shares to be in public hands. This is called the 'free float' and refers to shares owned by someone other than the founders or controlling shareholders. (Some companies can get round this requirement if they are sufficiently large. The key is that a large number of shares should be tradable, so that the shares will be liquid.)

Companies also have the option of joining the Alternative Investment Market (AIM) or the Techmark. The Techmark forum was set up by the London Stock Exchange in late 1999 to try to ensure that hi-tech companies did not desert London for other more favourable locations. There are less onerous restrictions than for companies that want to float on the main market. However, it is not a completely separate market. Many long-established main market companies are now also classed as Techmark stocks. Those that join the Techmark are not required to have a three-year trading record but have to produce quarterly results if they do not. They must be valued at a minimum of £50 million when they float and 25 per cent of the shares must be tradable in a free float.

On the Alternative Investment Market (AIM) there are very few requirements for companies: no trading record, no minimum level of free float, no minimum size. The onus is placed on the company's nominated adviser, who is required to decide whether the company is suitable to join the market and to make sure it follows the rules once it has done so.

AIM companies are required to inform shareholders of any change in the holdings of directors or individuals concerned with the company, the departure and appointment of directors, new share issues and the resignation or dismissal of the appointed adviser. An AIM company that fails to meet the above requirements could find its share quote suspended or even cancelled.

It costs a lot less to join AIM than the main market, with the base cost only around £250,000–£300,000, according to the Stock Exchange. The idea is to attract young and fast-growing companies to the market. But the result is that AIM companies are higher risk than main market companies. In these circumstances, a lot of responsibility is put on the adviser and broker who bring the company to market. A broker with a poor new issue record in the past will not attract funds for new companies.

TYPES OF SHARES

All companies within a sector are not the same and thus all shares do not offer the same kind of opportunities and risks.

Before you buy shares, you should ask yourself what type of investment you want: high growth? conservative growth? high income? Among the most common types of shares are:

CLASSIFICATION BY STAGE OF THE COMPANY'S GROWTH

Growth stocks These are shares in companies in high-growth industries or in established industries expanding into new areas. Stocks in the technology, mobile telephone and biotechnology industries are obvious examples. But high growth can come from unexpected areas: Matalan has been one of the fastest growing businesses over recent years although it has been involved in the 'old-fashioned' business of selling women's clothing.

High-growth companies will not normally pay much in the way of a dividend; some will not pay a dividend at all. That is because the companies will be putting as much of their cash as possible back into the business. Growth shares will also be highly rated relative to the company's current profits because investors are anticipating rapid growth in the future. They expect this growth to be reflected directly in the price increase of the shares. This also makes growth shares risky. Their prices may fall quickly, rather than rise, if the company's prospects change.

High-yielding shares also called income shares. These shares will pay a high dividend relative to the company's share price; in percentage terms, this return can be as high as the interest available on a building society account.

High-yielding shares are usually in businesses that are long-established and are not expected to grow that much in the future. One example would be the water industry: Britons are unlikely suddenly to use 20 per cent more water than before. But it is still a profitable industry and the companies can afford to pay out a good return to shareholders.

Cyclical stocks These are the shares of businesses whose fortunes tend to go up and down in line with the economic cycle. When the economy is booming, they do extremely well; when the economy is in recession, they suffer. One obvious example is construction companies; people stop building new offices and houses when times are hard. Cyclical shares can be very volatile. The trick is to buy them when times are bad and the share price is low, and to sell them when times are good and the price is high.

Penny shares These are shares with a very low share price, under 50p or £1, and they are notoriously risky. Most penny shares belong to small companies. Some investors erroneously think that penny shares represent good value because they are cheap, whereas what matters is the profits and assets that back the share concerned, not the share price.

Recovery shares These are shares in companies that have temporarily hit bad times. It could be that the company has suffered a disaster: a fire at a plant, a strike or a punitive lawsuit. It could be that it has made a disastrous foray into some new line of business. The key is that the problems are temporary. Eventually, the company will solve its problems, perhaps with the help of new management. When it does, the share price will recover from its lows.

But on top of the above differences, it is worth remembering that most shares are classed by the industry the company belongs to (see Figure 2.1). You can see the groupings in the back pages of the *Financial Times*. There are obvious groupings such as retailers and construction but there are also less clear ones such as support services, and portmanteau categories such as restaurants, pubs and breweries.

Sectors go in and out of fashion but it is useful, when picking stocks, to compare one company with another in the same sector. You might have decided to buy a pharmaceuticals stock but does that mean you buy GlaxoSmithKline or Astra Zeneca?

CLASSIFICATION BY INDEX

Companies on the UK stock market are classified into various indices, designed to help investors follow the main trend in an industry and compare similar companies with each other. These fall into two broad groups: the size-based index and the sector-based index.

FTSE 30 or FT Ordinary index is the oldest index dating back to 1935. It is designed to include some of the UK's best-known corporate names and was a widely used benchmark until the FTSE 100 was introduced in 1984. It is now little used.

FTSE 100 The best-known size-based index is the FTSE 100 (or 'Footsie' for short). FTSE is a classification company jointly owned by the *Financial Times* and the London Stock

Figure 2.1 Sector-based Indices

RESOURCES	BASIC INDUSTRIES	GENERAL INDUSTRIALS	CYCLICAL CONSUMER GOODS	NON-CYCLICAL CONSUMER GOODS
mining, oil & gas	chemicals, construction & building materials, forestry & paper, steel & other metals	aerospace & defence, diversified industrials, electronic & electronic equipment, engineering & machinery	automobiles, household goods & textiles	beverages, food producers & processors, health, packaging, personal care & household products, pharmaceuticals, tobacco

Exchange. The FTSE 100 aims to capture the 100 largest companies on the market. But, in fact, it never quite meets that goal. FTSE is re-balanced every three months. Companies that have fallen in value are dropped out of the index and those that have risen are added in. In the intervening period, however, there will be times when companies are in the FTSE but are only, say, the 115th largest company in the UK. (Changes can occur in between meetings if an index constituent is taken over.)

When the committee meets, it follows two main rules. The first is that any company that is among the 90 largest quoted groups in the UK must be included in the index. The second is that any company that is not one of the 110 largest groups must drop out. With luck, the two groups will match. If not, then either the largest available company will be included or the smallest current constituents will drop out. The aim of the rules is to make index changes transparent so that any

CYCLICAL SERVICES	NON-CYCLICAL SERVICES	UTILITIES	INFORMATION TECHNOLOGY	FINANCIALS
distributors, general retailers, leisure, entertainment & hotels, media & photography, pubs, support services, transport	food & drug retailers, telecommunication services	electricity, gas distribution, water	hardware & software, computer services	banks, insurance, life assurance, investment companies, real estate, speciality & other finance

fund aiming to track the index can have a reasonable antici-pation of index changes before they occur.

FTSE 250 The next index down from the FTSE 100 is the FTSE 250, sometimes known as the MidCap index. This aims to reflect the performance of the next 250 largest companies in the UK stock market; it contains some of the successful up-and-coming groups as well as previous industrial giants that are past their best.

FTSE 350 The above two indices are lumped together as the FTSE 350, although this is a little-used benchmark.

FTSE SmallCap The next index down is the FTSE SmallCap which contains smaller quoted companies. It has around 450 or so constituents.

FTSE All-Share The combination of the FTSE 100, 250 and SmallCap indices is known as the FTSE All-Share index. This is a widely used benchmark and tends to be used as a compar-ison by pension funds or unit trusts when they are trying to compare their performance with that of the market. Despite its name, the All-Share does not include every share on the stock market. It only has 800 or so out of the around 2,500 quoted groups. But in terms of market value, the All-Share does cover all but 1–2 per cent of the market; the remaining 1,700 quoted companies are very small. Indeed, the stock market is highly concentrated. The FTSE 100 makes up more than 80 per cent of the market.

There are other indices that cover the minnows of the stock market. The Fledgling index includes companies that are too small to be included in the SmallCap and the AIM index features those companies quoted on the Alternative Investment Market.

SECTOR-BASED INDICES
FTSE also classifies companies by the industry or type of

business they work in. The market is first divided into ten economic groups as shown in Figure 2.1, each of which consists of more than one sector.

These sectors vary substantially in size, both in terms of market value and number of companies. The big sectors in terms of market value are telecoms, oil, banks and pharmaceuticals. In each of those industries the UK has at least one company that ranks among the biggest in the world.

CHAPTER THREE

UNIT TRUSTS AND OEICS: POOLED INVESTMENTS

WHEN you buy shares in only one company, you are risking that something unexpected could happen – a strike, a fire at a factory, a lawsuit, fraud – to hurt your precious investment. To limit that risk, experts recommend that investors build a *diversified portfolio* of different kinds of shares. In other words, don't put all your eggs into one basket.

This is common sense, but even this sort of advice can cause confusion among inexperienced investors. Many people, for example, assume that in order to diversify their portfolio they must own shares in dozens – or even hundreds – of companies. I believe that investing in ten to fifteen companies in different business sectors is sufficient to protect you against *stock-specific* or *unsystematic risk* – the risk you run when you put all your money into one firm.

Diversifying your portfolio is not difficult. When I first began investing I decided to concentrate on high-tech stocks, but I soon discovered that not all high-tech stocks are the same. Indeed, 'high-tech' is a blanket term that covers a huge number of companies in a wide range of markets. Each business area within the high-tech sector – computer makers, chip makers, software companies, retailers, and so on – has its own strengths and weaknesses. So, by investing in several kinds of high-tech companies I was able to diversify my portfolio while keeping to my decision to invest in only one area.

You should also bear in mind *sector risk* – the risk that some unforeseen event or trend could adversely affect an entire business category. In the old days, for example, those who invested in sailing ships faced a sector risk with the emergence of steamships and railways.

Today, there seems to be an annual, mid-year correction in the computer market as a number of factors converge: school lets out, corporations undertake mid-year budget reviews, consumers go on holiday, etc. These summer doldrums are usually followed by a brisk recovery in the autumn. Once I figured this trend out, I understood that I should diversify into businesses that do not suffer from the mid-summer blues.

Diversifying your portfolio can chew up a lot of your time and money. You must be prepared to do the research – read the news about companies you invest in, look at share performance charts, and ask questions – necessary to understand which sectors go up or down, when and why. Also, if you take on ten sets of shares, you will be responsible for ten sets of dealing costs and will have to monitor the fortunes of ten different companies over the long term. If you haven't the time, patience or inclination for this, then you might consider investing in *unit trusts*.

Unit trusts (and investment trusts, which we'll cover in the next chapter) deliver investors a diversified portfolio at far less cost than the average person could achieve on their own. Indeed, investors don't even need to start with a lump sum.

They can put as little as £20 a month into a unit trust savings scheme.

Unit trusts don't avoid risk altogether, of course. If the stock market drops by 20 per cent, then the average unit trust will fall in value. But they do reduce the risk that a calamity at a single company will seriously damage your wealth. Another name for a unit trust is a *fund*. (In the US, the same kind of investment is known as a *mutual fund*.)

How do unit trusts work?

The word 'trust' can be a little bit off-putting, making it sound like one of those complicated inheritance devices you always read about in Victorian novels. In reality, a unit trust is just a big pool of money that is held on the investors' behalf by a trustee. Professional fund managers decide how the money should be invested. In such an arrangement, the trustee ensures that the money and shares are secure and that the fund manager does not do anything rash – such as putting 50 per cent of the money in one stock or switching the focus of the fund from the UK to Brazil.

Instead of owning individual shares, investors get 'units' in the fund. As the value of the portfolio rises, so does the value of the units. Imagine a fund with 10 million units, each priced at £1. The fund would be worth £10 million. If the value of the shares in the fund rose by 10 per cent, to £11 million, then the value of the units would also rise by 10 per cent to £1.10.

The size of the trust can change in two ways. First, the value of the investments in the trust will rise and fall, altering the overall value of the portfolio. In those circumstances the number of units in the trust will remain unchanged. Second, when investors buy and sell units, the trust changes size. If there are more buyers than sellers, the unit trust's manager will create more units, so the fund will expand. The manager will then go out and invest that new cash in the stock market. Conversely, if there are more sellers than buyers, then the manager will be forced to cancel or redeem units. In that case, the manager will have to pay out cash to those investors who redeem, and possibly sell some shares within the portfolio. (Most managers keep some cash reserves to meet redemptions. But if the selling is heavy enough, they will be forced to dip into their shareholdings.)

As an investor in a unit trust you can sell your holdings at any time during a normal stock market trading day and be assured of receiving the asset value of the fund. (As with any stock market investment, however, there is no guarantee that you will get your original money back.) You cannot, however, buy or sell units of the trust in the stock market yourself. You can only buy or sell from the unit trust manager, although an adviser or stockbroker can deal on your behalf.

The idea behind unit trusts is nice and simple, but unfortunately some of the terminology associated with it can be daunting. Similar vehicles are known as *open-ended investment companies* (OEICs), or *undertakings for collective investments in transferable securities* (UCITS). Regardless of how complicated the verbiage, if you remember that your units rise and fall in line with the value of the fund you won't go far wrong.

FEES

Everything has its price. While unit trusts can offer a cheap route to diversification, that doesn't mean they will do it for free. Fund managers want their cut of the deal, and they take it in two different ways: through the initial charge and the annual charge.

INITIAL CHARGE

When you first buy a unit trust, you'll pay the *initial charge*, which is a percentage of the money you invest. Typically, this is 5 per cent, although initial charges vary between fund managers and between funds. So if you make an investment of £1,000, then £50 (£1000 × 5%) immediately goes to the unit trust manager.

The charge can be imposed in two ways. The traditional approach is to have two different prices, a price at which you buy units (*the offer*) and a price at which you sell (*the bid*). Suppose you agreed to buy units in the Acme trust. By ringing the manager (or looking in some newspapers, such as the *Financial Times*), you can get an indication of the prices. Say that the offer price is 100p and the bid price is 94p. If you put in £1,000, you will get 1,000 units. But the immediate resale value of your units would be just £940 (1,000 units multiplied by the bid price of 94p).

The sharp-eyed of you will have noticed that the difference between £1,000 and £940 is 6 per cent, not 5 per cent. This is because the initial charge is not the only cost you have to bear. The manager also incurs costs when he invests more money on behalf of the fund. Shares also have two different prices: an offer and a bid. So when the manager invests your £1,000, the immediate resale value of the stocks he buys may only be £990. He passes those costs immediately on to you.

Many in the unit trust industry have thought that the business of having separate offer and bid prices was confusing to the average investor. So now there is an alternative fund structure, called an open-ended investment company (OEIC). The good news is that an OEIC is simple; the bad news is that it doesn't save you any money.

Under an OEIC, there is just one price at which you buy and sell. But when you make a purchase, you pay a separate set of

Gartmore Fund Managers (1200)F
Gartmore House, 8 Fenchurch Place, London EC3M 4PH
Dealings :0870 6016103   Inv Serv: Freephone 0800289336

UK Growth Funds

UK Selected Opps Inc. 5¼	74.04	78.68	+1.05	0.08
UK Selected Opps Acc 5¼	74.24	78.89	+1.05	0.08
Mastertrust Acc 3½	116.24	121.38	+1.60	0.41
Mastertrust Acc 3½	119.96	125.26	+1.65	0.41
Practical Inv Inc 5¼	153.58	166.28	+0.73	2.84
Do (Accum)............. 5¼	417.03	451.52	+1.97	2.84
Stable Growth 0	£100.00	100.00	....	0
UK Index Inc..................	244.63	245.86	+2.89	2.11
UK Index Acc...............	255.47	256.76	+3.03	2.11
UK & Irish Smlr Cos Inc 5¼	219.96	235.26	−0.15	0.35
UK & Irish Smlr Cos Acc 5¼	234.87	251.20	−0.16	0.35
UK Smaller Cos Inc .. 5¼	288.11	308.14	+0.26	0.00
UK Smaller Cos Acc . 5¼	289.67	309.81	+0.26	0.00
UK Growth Inc......... 5¼	91.96	98.03	+1.09	0.15
UK Growth Acc........ 5¼	103.95	110.81	+1.22	0.15
UK Techtornado 5¼	33.54	35.88	+0.52	0.00
UK Focus 5¼	97.05	103.79	+1.18	0.30

Income Funds

CashTrust **...............	181.07xd	181.07	+0.02	4.91
Corporate Bond Inc .. 3⅝	26.72	27.86	+0.04	5.54
Corporate Bond Acc . 3⅝	30.19	31.47	+0.04	5.54
UK Income Inc 5¼	46.10	49.17	+0.46	3.28
UK Income Acc 5¼	50.06	53.40	+0.50	3.28
Global Bond Inc....... 3⅝	28.62xd	29.69	+0.12	2.84
Global Bond Acc 3⅝	31.09xd	32.24	+0.13	2.84
UK Gilt & Fxd Int Inc. 3⅝	50.62xd	52.52	+0.01	4.42
UK Gilt & Fxd Int Acc 3⅝	77.72xd	80.64	+0.01	4.42
UK Growth & Income Inc . 5¼	222.21	236.46	+2.39	2.98
UK Growth & Inc Acc 5¼	238.76	254.08	+2.57	2.98
Corporate High Yld Bd Inc 3⅝	86.86	90.63	−0.38	9.05
Corporate High Yld Bd Acc . 3⅝	98.83	103.12	−0.44	9.05

International Funds

Emerging Markets Inc 5¼	44.49	47.42	+0.10	0.00
Emerging Markets Acc 5¼	44.57	47.51	+0.11	0.00
Global Utilities Inc 5¼	284.36xd	301.09	+2.57	0.10
Global Utilities Acc.... 5¼	286.20xd	303.04	+2.59	0.10
Global Balanced Inc.. 5¼	203.01	214.56	+1.40	0.11
Global Balanced Acc 5¼	203.40	214.97	+1.40	0.11
Global Growth Inc 5¼	140.23	148.38	+1.25	0.00
Global Growth Acc ... 5¼	140.23	148.38	+1.25	0.00
Global Focus............. 5¼	90.83	96.14	+0.84	0.00

Overseas Funds

American Growth Inc . 5¼	391.21xd	412.86	+1.54	0.00
American Growth Acc 5¼	391.21xd	412.86	+1.54	0.00
American Focus 5¼	86.70	91.50	−0.21	0.00
European Growth Inc.. 5¼	238.79	253.03	+3.28	0.00
European Growth Acc 5¼	238.79	253.03	+3.28	0.00
European Focus........ 5¼	79.05	83.81	+0.77	0.00
Euro Sel Opps 5¼	463.00	490.71	+5.18	0.00
American Smaller Cos Inc. 5¼	320.01	338.46	+1.00	0.00
American Smaller Cos Acc. 5¼	320.01	338.46	+1.00	0.00
China Growth Inc 5¼	166.29	177.34	+2.89	0.30
China Growth Acc 5¼	168.17	179.34	+2.92	0.30
Japanese Growth Inc . 5¼	206.86xd	218.43	+6.98	0.00
Japanese Growth Acc 5¼	206.86xd	218.43	+6.98	0.00
Japan Focus 5¼	88.84	93.80	+2.70	0.00
Pacific Growth Inc.... 5¼	157.52xd	167.90	+2.31	0.00
Pacific Growth Acc... 5¼	158.83xd	169.30	+2.34	0.00

Figure 3.1 The illustration shows a typical unit trust listing in the *Financial Times*. The top line shows the name of the fund manager and the F indicates that the trust operates on a forward pricing basis. Below that are the company's address and phone numbers.

Financial Times, July 2001

charges on top, the manager's initial charge and any additional costs he chooses to pass on. So if you want to put £1,000 into an Acme OEIC, you will probably have to invest £1,060, with the extra £60 representing the charges. Six per cent is a pretty big chunk of your money. That could easily represent your first year's profit from investing in the fund. So it follows that you should not invest in a unit trust or OEIC unless you are willing to leave your money in for at least a year. And if you allow for the ups and downs of the market, you probably want to think of a unit trust as a five-year investment.

To be fair to the unit trust manager, not all of the initial charge goes directly to the management group itself. If you buy your unit trust through a financial adviser, they will receive part of the initial charge (normally 3 per cent of the value of your investment) as commission. Unit trust companies have found that paying this charge to advisers and brokers is a highly effective way of getting more investors, and thus more money into their funds.

There are ways of avoiding paying the whole initial charge. *Discount brokers* will sell you unit trusts for a one-off fee, which works out at less than the initial charge. They will not give you any advice, however, which means you will have to pick your funds yourself. There are also some fee-based financial advisers who do not take commission. Like a lawyer or accountant, they give paid advice by the hour. They rebate any commissions received to the investor. If you are investing a substantial sum, you could find that the adviser's fee is more than offset by the commission savings you make. Finally, if you are investing a substantial sum (over £10,000), and you buy directly from the unit trust company, you may find that the company will be willing to reduce the initial charge. The more you invest, the lower the charge or the more that rebate could be.

ANNUAL CHARGE

The second type of fee imposed by the unit trust manager is the *annual charge*. This is not a fee that you pay directly. A unit trust manager deducts the annual charge from the value of the whole fund every year. But it is just as important a cost as the initial charge. And if you own a unit trust for a number of years the annual charge is probably more important because it is a recurring charge rather than a one-off.

Annual charges tend to fall into the range of 1–1.5 per cent. Let's return to Acme trust. It has 100 million units, worth £1 each, so the overall fund is worth £100 million. Over the course of the year the fund manager will take out its 1 per cent fee, equivalent to £1 million. That means that if the fund does not grow at all, then the total value of the fund will be just £99 million. Your £1 unit is now worth just 99p. That doesn't sound so bad. But let's assume that the stock market returns 10 per cent every year. If the manager takes a charge of 1 per cent every year, that cuts the investor's return to 9 per cent, a fall of a tenth.

The larger the fee the greater its impact will be on your return. That makes a big difference over the long term. One thousand pounds invested for ten years at 10 per cent will grow to £2,593. At 9 per cent, the final sum falls to £2,367 and at 8.5 per cent, just £2,261. Throw in the 5 per cent initial charge, and you can see how your returns can really be eaten away by the manager's fees.

OTHER CHARGES

And there are yet more fees to pay. The manager will also pass on fees for services, such as custody (a charge for the safekeeping of share certificates) and stockbroking commissions. It all adds up, and it isn't easy to find out what your total costs will be before you invest. (At some point the industry may publish a *total expense ratio* for each fund, but it hasn't happened yet.)

With all this talk of fees and managers, you might be thinking that owning a unit trust is a rip-off. But that is far from true. After all, you'd face some of these same costs if you invested the money yourself, and you'd have to spend a lot of time and money following the stock market as closely as a unit trust manager does. So, at the end of the day, a unit trust is a good starting point for novice investors.

If the stock market enjoys a bull run (a period in which overall share prices are rising) – as it has for much of the time since 1982 – then the effect of charges can be minimal compared to the profits earned by unit trust investors. Indeed, the average UK equity unit trust gained 207.5 per cent during the 1990s, a compound return of almost 12 per cent a year. That's a lot more than an investor would have received from a building society.

Nevertheless, you should look closely at charges when you come to consider a unit trust manager. All things being equal, it is best to pick a manager with the lowest charges. If one fund has an annual fee of 1 per cent and another 1.5 per cent, and you pick the cheaper one, then you'll have a 0.5 per cent a year head start over those who invest in the second fund. And over the long term that can add up to a significant advantage.

PERFORMANCE

While it is often true that performance outweighs fees, it is also worth noting that fees are known in advance while performance is not. Fund management companies love to shower you with statistics demonstrating how their fund is one of the best performers of the last few years. But these reports always come with the disclaimer 'Past performance is no guide to the future.' And that is the truth – as the many formerly high-flying fund managers who have stumbled in recent years can attest. The funds that are top of their sector one year are not guaranteed to be in the same place the following year.

You should be very careful about buying a fund on the back of one good year. At the very least, check performance statistics to see how the fund has done over longer periods, such as three or five years. Look also to see if the same fund manager has been in charge all the time. A fund might have a hot record over five years, but if the manager has quit for another job those figures are much less meaningful.

Another statistic to consider is the *risk rating* of the fund, which describes how variable the performance of the funds is likely to be.

You could put your money into a building society and earn a steady 5 per cent a year. But that's not a very exciting return. To get a higher return, you need to take on some risk. The higher the return you want, the more risk you have to be prepared to take. This is the fundamental law of finance.

The same principle applies to fund managers. Some will stick to safe and steady shares, such as BP and Tesco, while others may go for riskier fare, such as Internet companies or biotechnology groups. The latter group of managers might have a very good year from time to time, but they will also have some terrible years as well. In financial jargon, the unit trust they manage will have *greater volatility*.

Academics have come up with statistics that check how a fund's performance compares with its risk profile. The best known is called the *Sharpe ratio*. It compares the volatility of the fund with its growth. In theory, top fund managers will produce above-average performance with below-average risk. You may find it difficult to get Sharpe ratios for funds.

But the companies that track the performance of unit trusts, such as Micropal, do publish figures on the volatility of funds. You can find them on the Internet at *www.micropal.com*.

Investors should also be careful about looking at absolute returns. It is not uncommon for a business sector to have a hot year, and show a 100 per cent return. But this is rare, and should be viewed as the exception rather than the rule. When the fund manager advertises that kind of statistic, it looks really tempting – wouldn't we all like to double our money in one year? – but I recommend healthy scepticism. It's highly unlikely that if you buy into that fund you'll earn 100 per cent over the following year, and it is absolutely certain that you won't see such a return every year.

TYPES OF TRUSTS

As of this writing, there are almost 1,800 unit trusts to choose from in the UK. And within this large pool there are many varieties of trust. Some invest in a particular industry, such as technology; some in a particular type of share, such as recovery stocks; some aim for a higher than usual income; some invest in overseas markets. This means you can find almost any type of investment you want, but the choice can seem bewildering.

The first choice you have to make is between an *actively managed fund* and an *index-tracker fund*. An active manager selects shares on the basis of their analysis. An index-tracker simply attempts to match the performance of an index such as the FTSE 100.

Many assume that the choice between these two types of investment is easy: surely a good fund manager should be able to beat the index, their thinking goes. But the fact of the matter is that most sophisticated, highly paid managers do not – indeed *cannot* – beat the lowly clerk who oversees an index.

Over the five years to 31 December 2000, the average UK All Companies unit trust gained 85.6 per cent, compared with a total return from the FTSE All-Share index of 91.7 per cent.

Why do fund managers find it so hard to beat the index? Certain academics use the efficient markets theory to maintain it is impossible for individual investors to 'beat' the market consistently over the long term. According to this theory, all the available information about an asset is already reflected in the current price. Therefore attempting to make profits on the basis of that information is fruitless. The only thing that can move the share price up or down is new information. However, unless you have a crystal ball, that cannot be known in advance.

Let me explain how this theory affects you. Supposing you see on the *Six O'Clock News* that sales at Sainsbury's have increased strongly over the last year. You say to yourself: the company is obviously doing well, but should I rush out and buy Sainsbury's shares? Well, not necessarily. According to the efficient markets theory, traders on the Stock Exchange would have seen the news about Sainsbury's as soon as it was announced, and marked up the price accordingly. Even doing complicated calculations involving price-earnings ratios and dividend yields would not help. Other people would have done the calculations before you, and bought or sold shares accordingly. The market, therefore, is so efficient that it is impossible to beat.

A lot of people who manage money for a living scorn the efficient markets theory. That's not surprising: the theory implies that their jobs are very nearly pointless. But the facts are stark: almost all managers eventually under-perform the index. Indeed, it is inevitable that they do so. Professional fund managers – those who run unit trusts, pension funds and insurance companies – own the bulk of the stock market.

Given that the index represents the average performance of the market, then it should also represent the average performance of fund managers. But the index does not have any costs. Fund managers, on the other hand, must pay commissions every time they buy and sell shares, and they must also pay the spread between the bid and offer prices. Because of these operating costs, they are doomed to under-perform an index.

There have been superstar investors such as Warren Buffett and George Soros, who have beaten the index for years at a time, but even these financial superheroes have stumbled recently. And there are not enough of these above-average managers to prove decisively that investing success is due to good judgement rather than luck.

INDEX-TRACKING FUNDS (AKA TRACKER FUNDS)

An index-tracking fund is a portfolio of shares whose performance moves in tandem with a designated measure of the market such as the FTSE 100 or the performance of a given sector. These funds deliberately try to match the performance of the index, either by buying all the constituents, or those that in the past have closely tracked the index. Index funds have costs, but these are limited: they only need to buy and sell shares when index constituents change, or when investors take money in and out of the fund. This means that such funds under-perform the index itself by a fraction of a percentage point.

Active fund managers, in contrast, expend a lot of effort trying to find the shares that will be winners and dump the ones they expect to be losers. This requires a lot of trading – some managers turn over their portfolios several times a year – which translates into a lot of costs and reduced returns for investors.

Cost is a big factor in favour of index-trackers. Not only

do they have lower dealing costs, they charge investors much lower fees. There are no expensive managers to pay, since the composition of the portfolio can be calculated by computer.

Whereas active managers usually impose an initial charge of 5 per cent, some index-tracking funds have no initial charge. And the annual fee can be as little as 0.5 per cent, compared with an average of 1–1.5 per cent for most unit trusts. The overall effect is that when you invest in a tracking fund more of your money is working for you and less is going into the pocket of the managers.

Note, however, that because an index-tracking fund has low charges, it does not normally pay commissions to brokers and advisers. As a result, you may well find that your financial adviser will not recommend an index fund for the simple reason that there is nothing in it for them. This is one of the reasons why the commission system is bad news for investors: it creates a conflict of interest between the adviser and the client.

An index-tracking fund is highly unlikely to be the best performing trust in its sector. Instead it is more than likely to be better than average, and very unlikely to be the worst performing fund. At the end of the day, you will do neither better nor worse than the market, but that will be better than roughly 80 per cent of actively managed funds in the UK and in the US.

ACTIVELY MANAGED FUNDS

Most index funds are found in just one sector of the unit trust market – UK equity funds – but there are lots of other types of trust available, and in most cases they are run by active managers. If you choose the right fund, and the market is relatively healthy, then you can do quite well by investing in one of the following types of funds.

Equity income funds These trusts buy shares with a higher-than-average dividend yield. They pay investors a modest income, better than that available on growth funds, but normally well below that available from a building society. In theory they will offer less scope for capital gain than a conventional fund. But in the past there have been periods when equity income funds have provided a higher total return than growth funds. This happens when buying high-yielding shares has been a successful stock-picking strategy.

Small company funds These trusts invest in shares of companies that have not made it into the FTSE 100 index. Investing in smaller companies has proved a pretty good strategy over the long run; smaller companies have a greater potential for growth than established groups. But they are also more risky, since the failure of one product or the loss of a few key customers can damage their business severely.

Emerging market funds These trusts invest in company shares in a range of developing economies known as emerging markets: South-East Asia, Latin America and Eastern Europe, for example. These economies are growing fast. And in theory the returns from companies that operate in emerging markets should be better over the long run. In practice, however, emerging market economies are less stable, have greater political risk and lower standards of investor protection. Emerging market funds tend to produce a highly volatile performance and are considered a high-risk investment.

Individual country funds There are a host of these. In some cases they focus on a single big market, such as the US or Japan; in other cases they are based on a very small market, such as Thailand or South Korea. The latter type of fund is high-risk and should only be considered by investors who have already built up substantial holdings in the UK and other major markets.

International funds These funds invest in a broad range of stocks that trade on the international markets, including, in some cases, huge multinational companies that trade on the UK Stock Exchange. They give the investor a chance to participate in some of the world's other main markets, such as the US and Japan, without the risk of being concentrated in one area. International funds are a good investment for people who have already built up an exposure to the UK market and are looking to diversify their holdings.

Regional funds These trusts invest in shares within a particular geographical region. The biggest sector is Europe, which is the UK's biggest trading partner and a region that is becoming increasingly integrated by the euro. Other regional funds are variations of emerging market funds that focus on Asia or Latin America.

Sectoral funds These trusts invest purely in one industrial sector of the market. The most popular recent example has been technology funds. Sectoral funds can deliver very high returns if the sector happens to be performing well, but they are highly volatile and represent a risky investment as 2001 proved.

Ethical funds These trusts avoid companies to which some people have moral objections, including tobacco companies, firms that conduct animal testing or sell arms. If you are concerned about the ethical implications of your investments, then check carefully that a fund you are considering operates in accordance with your beliefs. For example, some ethical funds may invest in businesses even if they earn a small proportion of their profits from, say, gambling; you may want a fund that is 100 per cent pure.

Gilt funds These unit trusts invest in the bonds issued by the UK government, popularly known as gilt-edged securities, or gilts, because of the virtual certainty that they will be repaid. They will deliver a reliable income, but investors should not expect much, if any, capital growth. Gilt funds are best for those, often the retired, who need safe, dependable income.

Corporate bond funds These trusts invest in the bonds issued by big companies: they offer a higher income than is available from a gilt fund, but that comes with a correspondingly higher risk. (Some of the companies involved might go bankrupt, or fail to keep up with their bond payments.) Again, investors should not expect much capital growth, and the higher the potential income the greater the risk of capital loss. They are suitable for investors who need a high level of income in the short term and are willing to accept a risk.

Global Bond Funds These trusts invest in bonds from all over the world. Their biggest investments tend to be in bonds issued by overseas governments, such as the US, Germany or Japan. They add an additional opportunity for gain or loss. The value of the fund will rise if the pound falls against overseas currencies, and fall if the pound rises. Global bond funds are suitable for investors who already have a UK bond fund and are looking to diversify.

Commodity funds These trusts invest in the shares of companies that produce commodities, such as mining groups. They have been poor performers in recent years as commodity prices have been weak. But they are a useful option for those investors who believe that inflation is set to return in a big way, and want to hedge their bets.

Currency funds These trusts shift money between various overseas currencies. As they do not invest in equities, they tend to offer limited growth but a decent income.

Cash or money market funds These trusts invest in short-term securities issued by banks and other creditworthy borrowers. They represent an alternative to a building society account. While they will never pay the highest rate in the market, they should always offer a reasonably competitive return. They charge lower fees than conventional unit trusts.

Funds of funds These trusts invest in a range of other unit trusts. As a consequence, they offer a less volatile return than can be obtained from an individual unit trust. But the charges are high, since the investor is paying two sets of fees: one to the manager of the fund of funds, and another to the managers of the underlying trusts.

Protected funds These offer investors a chance to invest in the stock market but with some security. For example, an investor might receive 80 per cent of the rise in the FTSE All-Share index with a guarantee of their money back after five years. These may be suitable for first-time investors who are nervous about losing some of their capital. But it is worth considering that the stock market goes up over the majority of five-year periods so the guarantee will not normally be needed. So investors may be giving away a lot of return in order to pay for unnecessary protection.

INDIVIDUAL SAVINGS ACCOUNTS (ISAS)

All of the above unit trusts represent an abundance of choice for investors. But you can also choose to hold your unit trusts within an *individual savings account*, or ISA. An ISA is a tax-efficient savings vehicle established by the government in the 1999–2000 tax year; it replaces the old *personal equity plan*, or PEP.

ISAs are available in a rather confusing variety of forms. You can choose between a maxi-ISA or three mini-ISAs, covering shares, cash and insurance. In most cases, it is best to opt for a maxi-ISA, as this gives you the maximum amount of flexibility. Up to £7,000 can be put into a maxi-ISA in the

2001–02 tax year. There is no minimum holding period for such an investment.

It is easy to get confused by the terminology. Many companies will advertise their 'Technology ISA' or 'UK Equity ISA'. If you are still putting your money into a unit trust, you could invest in the same trust without the ISA wrapping. The trust exists independent of the ISA. So even if you have used up your annual £7,000 ISA allowance, you can put more money in the same fund. The only differences are:

The tax treatment Any capital growth made within an ISA is free of capital gains tax (CGT). It is worth pointing out that, in any case, every individual can gain up to a certain sum (£7,500 in the 2001–02 tax year) without paying any CGT. Most people go through their lives without paying CGT. You might think you will never make a gain of that size. But why aim low? If you made an investment of £5,000, and it tripled over three years, you would be disappointed if you had to hand over some of your windfall to the taxman.

Interest income earned within an ISA is tax-free. So, if you need income, cash funds and corporate bond funds can be an attractive option for an ISA investment. Investors in an ISA get a tax credit of 10 per cent on dividend income. This relief is scheduled to end in 2004. The tax credit is quite a complicated notion. It derives from the fact that companies have to pay tax on their profits before they pay dividends to shareholders. Some investors, such as pension funds, have traditionally not been liable for tax. So they were entitled to claim back the notional tax they paid on their dividend income.

In the Labour government's first budget Gordon Brown abolished the tax credit for most investors. But he did allow the tax credit to remain for ISA investors (and for remaining PEP holdings). So let's assume that the unit trust manager pays a dividend of 9p a unit: thanks to the 10 per cent tax credit, the dividend would be rounded up by a penny to make 10p.

Fees In many cases, unit trust companies levy exactly the same charges for ISA investments as for non-ISA investments. In such cases, you might as well have your holding in ISA form because you get the tax benefits for nothing. Some fund managers actually impose lower charges on ISA investments, which makes the deal doubly attractive. But you should always watch closely to see if the trust manager imposes any *extra* charges on ISA investments. If it does, then chances are it may not be worth investing in ISA form since the charges may well outweight the tax benefits unless you are a regular CGT payer.

PURCHASING A UNIT TRUST

So you have finally decided to invest in a unit trust. How do you go about it?

You can go directly to the unit trust company itself. There is a comprehensive list of trusts in the Companies and Markets pages of the *Financial Times* and there are also listings in the City pages of most broadsheet newspapers. Those listings will give the phone numbers for the companies concerned. In addition, the fund management companies will advertise separately in the press, magazines or on posters. And some banks (such as Barclays) have their own ranges of trusts that you can buy through branches. Internet enthusiasts can also find plenty of unit trust information online. A good place to start is the all-purpose financial website *www.find.co.uk*.

As I mentioned earlier in this chapter, buying directly from the company may not be the cheapest route because of the initial charge. You may be able to get a better deal through a discount broker or a fee-charging financial adviser.

When you invest in a plain unit trust, you buy at the offer price, which includes an allowance for charges. When you invest in an OEIC, there is just one price, but you will pay the charges on top.

You may be offered a choice of unit types. In most cases, the choice is between *accumulation units* and *distribution* or *income units*. Income units pay income (and distribution units distribute it). Investors in accumulation units still get the same income, but instead of it being paid out, it is 'rolled up' into the price of a fund.

Say a unit trust offers both accumulation and income units of 100p. The first year it pays out income of 2p per unit (after tax). The holders of the income units get a cheque. The investors who have the accumulation unit see their unit price go up by 2p. They will receive the benefit of the income when they sell. The choice is yours, but it is probably best to buy the accumulation units unless you are retired or otherwise need the income. That way more of your money stays in the trust and gets the benefit of long-term growth.

PRICING

Unit trusts set their prices on either a historic or forward basis. A few fund management groups use historic prices based on the previous day's market close which means that you can find out the price in advance (it may even be the one in that morning's paper). The vast majority of trusts deal on a forward basis. This means you do not know the exact price you will pay. The price is set later, when the manager has been able to assess the value of the portfolio in the light of that day's market closing prices.

This may sound like you are buying a pig in a poke. But if the market falls that day, you may find you are paying a lower price than you would have paid on a historic price basis. Even if the price has risen, it should make precious little difference to your investment over the long run – unless the move is exceptional. And the long run is what matters. The consequence of buying units on a forward basis is that your best bet is to choose a lump sum that you wish to invest, whether it is £500 or £5,000. You will learn how many units you have bought, and at what price, when the unit trust company sends you a *contract note*. This will state the terms of the deal. Whether you have bought units on a historic or a forward basis, you will have to send off a cheque normally within four days.

Once you are a unit trust owner, you can follow the price of your units every day in the broadsheet press. Remember, you must always look at the bid price, the lower of the two. That's what you would get if you sell your holding. (With an OEIC, there is only one price to look at.)

The unit trust company will send you several bits of paper a year, including annual reports and proxies. If the unit trust pays dividends, you will receive dividend statements once or twice a year. These show the amount of dividend paid per unit and the total sum paid to you (or reinvested on your behalf, if you have opted for accumulation units). It will also include a mysterious figure called a *tax credit*. It is the amount of tax deducted from your dividend. You will need this information when you fill out your tax form. If you are a basic rate taxpayer, then the tax credit effectively discharges your tax liability; you will not have to pay any more. But if you are a higher rate taxpayer, then you will have to pay the difference between the basic rate and higher rate tax. The best news is if you are not a taxpayer (perhaps a non-working spouse whose savings income does not meet the basic tax threshold). You will be able to claim back the tax credit from the government, just as you can in an ISA or PEP.

The unit trust manager should also send you updates on the fund's progress. This should tell you how the price has performed, both in absolute terms and relative to an appropriate index. (In the UK this will probably be the FTSE All-Share.) It is worth a read. The commentary is usually intelligent and gives you an expert view of where the markets are going. Have a look at the back of the report as well, which should give you the fund's largest purchases and sales. Some trading is inevitable. But if you spot, for example, the same shares being bought and sold in a short period, the manager may be *churning* the portfolio. That is, every time he trades he gets a commission – and you incur a cost, which affects your returns. Unless there have been very turbulent market conditions, that is a bad sign.

UNIT TRUST SAVINGS SCHEMES

One of the beauties of unit trusts is that they offer the chance to benefit from stock market gains to the smallest of investors. You can build up a lump sum through a unit trust savings scheme. Each month, your investment is used to purchase units. Different companies have different rules on minimum investments but some allow investments as small as £20 a month.

Savings scheme investors have to pay exactly the same initial and annual charges as everyone else. But they get the benefit of what is known as *pound-cost averaging*. (This is explained in detail in chapter 8.) They buy fewer units when the price is high and more when it is low. Take the following example. You decide to put £50 a month into the Acme UK equity fund. In month one the stock market is high and Acme units are £1 each. You get 50 units. In the next month there is a stock market slump and the price falls to 80p. Your £50 buys 62.5 units. Then the price recovers back to £1 in month three. You get another 50 units. Over the three months as a whole, you have purchased 162.5 units. Ignoring charges for the purpose of this example, your holding is worth £162.5. Had you put in £150 at the start when the price was £1, your holding would still be worth just £150.

Pound-cost averaging doesn't always work as neatly as the above example. And it is worth noting that because equities tend to rise in price, investors with lump sums will normally do better to invest their lump sum at once rather than dribble it out through a savings scheme. On the other hand, there is nothing more disturbing to the first-time investor than to see the market fall 20 per cent just *after* you have finally plucked up courage to put your money into the market. Using a unit trust savings scheme means you avoid the risk of putting all in your money at the top of the market.

You might be pleasantly surprised to see how the small sums invested in a savings scheme add up. Had you invested £50 a month in a UK growth unit trust scheme at the start of the 1990s, for example, your investment would have been worth £13,320 by the end of 1999; that compares with a cumulative investment of £6,000.

What is especially nice about savings schemes is that you can effectively forget about them. Every month the money goes straight out of your bank account, and after a while you cease to notice. But you *will* notice a nice fat cheque when you cash in. It is a fairly painless way of saving.

CHAPTER FOUR

INVESTMENT TRUSTS

J UST like unit trusts, investment trusts give the small investor the chance to own a broad portfolio of shares at modest cost. They can be held in an individual savings account (ISA) and purchased via a savings scheme. But they have a quite different structure from their unitised cousins. And although this structure has some distinct advantages, this has led them to be a lot less popular in recent years.

Investment trusts date back to 1868, when Foreign & Colonial (F&C) was established to invest in overseas markets. F&C survives today as one of Britain's largest investment trusts. A number of trusts were set up in the late nineteenth century, particularly in Scotland, by solicitors and accountants who had been asked to look after clients' money. The trust structure made it a lot simpler to keep everyone's affairs in order, and allowed clients to see how their investments were performing. The original trusts invested heavily in overseas securities, often in countries that were then part of Britain's empire.

STRUCTURE

Investment trusts are quoted companies on the stock market just like British Telecom or Marks & Spencer. When you buy or sell shares in an investment trust, you do it through a stockbroker. This means the price is set by supply and demand, like everything else. Like all other companies, investment trusts have a board of directors who are responsible to shareholders. The board appoints a fund management group to manage the portfolio and agrees matters such as management fees and contract lengths. The structure of investment trusts has three important consequences.

(1) Because the share price is set by supply and demand, it does not automatically match the value of the assets in the portfolio which is called the net asset value. Computed each business day, it is the market value of all the securities in the portfolio minus any on-going expenses that the trust charges. This remainder is then divided by the fixed number of trust shares in issue. The market price of the trust's shares can be at discount to the net asset value (the normal situation). The share price can either be at a discount to the net asset value (the normal situation), at a premium to it, or equal (which is rarely the case). In other words, if the share price is 80p and the net asset value of the trust is 100p, the shares would be at a 20 per cent discount. If the shares were trading at 105p, they would be at a 5 per cent premium.

(2) The manager of an investment trust can be changed if the board (or shareholders) wish. If, for example, you buy shares in Fidelity's International unit trust, it will always be managed by Fidelity, but the board can throw out an investment trust manager if they are not performing well. This is even the case with those investment trusts (such as Perpetual Income) that have the manager's name as part of their title. If the board does not act, an outside investor may even mount a takeover bid in an attempt to have the manager removed.

(3) Unlike unit trusts, the size of an investment trust only

INVESTMENT COMPANIES

	Notes	Price	+ or –	52 week high	52 week low	Yield	NAV	Dis or Pm(-)
3i	✤♣	982xd	+25	1797	951	1.3	765.1	–28.4
3i Bioscience	♣	476	+1	757½	389	–	534.5	10.9
3i Euro Technology	♣	28	+2	136½	25¼	–	31.9	12.2
3i Smllr Quoted Cos	♣	192	+½	318	191½	2.3	240.9	20.3
3i UK Select		102	....	119	98½	2.7	111.1	8.2
3PC		101	....	101½	99½	–	96.8	–4.3
ACM Euro Enhanced		66½	....	106	66½	13.5	65.9	–.9
AIM Distribution		100	....	150	85	10.8	117.2	14.7
AIM Trust	♣	257½	+8	481½	249½	0.4	274.3	6.1
AIM VCT	s	175	....	238	150	0.8	163.6	–7.0
AIM VCT 2		90	....	120	75	–	95.1	5.4
Aberdeen Asian Smlr	♣	92½	+2	110¼	87	1.3	111.2	16.8
Warrants		29¼	+¼	47½	28¾	–	–	–
Aberdeen Convertible	♣	91xd	....	111	82	8.8	83.3	–9.2
Aberdeen Devlpt Capital	♣	62½xd	....	77½	60½	8.3	58.2	–7.3
Zero Div Pref		73½	....	76	63½	–	72.3	–1.7
Aberdeen Emrg Ecos	♣	61¼	–¼	78	59	–	74.2	17.5
Warrants		11½	–¾	22½	11½	–	–	–
Aberdeen High Inc	♣F	56½	+½	113	55½	17.7	45.2	–25.1
Aberdeen Latin Amer	♣	60¼	–½	77¼	55½	–	67.9	11.3
Warrants		11¼	–¼	23½	10	–	–	–
Aberdeen New Dawn	♣	169½	+1½	195½	163½	1.0	206.0	17.7
Aberdeen New Thai	♣	42½	–¾	45½	33½	1.6	49.6	14.4
Aberdeen Pfd	♣M	78½xd	+¼	147	77	24.5	45.5	–72.6
5⅜pc RPI Deb 2007		£114$\frac{23}{32}$	+⅛	£116$\frac{3}{32}$	£112$\frac{29}{32}$	4.7	–	–
Units 8 1/4pc Ln '23		£98⅞	+$\frac{27}{32}$	£105⅜	£96$\frac{27}{32}$	8.3	–	–
Aberdeen Pfd Zero Dv Pf		281	–½	281¾	258	–	277.4	–1.3
Aberdn Pf Scs ZDv Pf 08		107½	+½	111¾	101	–	106.0	–1.4
Aberforth Smllr		327¼	–¼	350½	255½	2.6	374.7	12.7
Warrants		230	+½	250	155	–	–	–
Aberforth Split Inc	†	54½	....	61	50	26.8	–	–
Cap		464½	+½	478	337	–	545.8	14.9
Units	†	518	....	530	386½	2.8	558.7	7.3
Acorn Income Fund	♣†	145	....	151	124½	7.9	137.7	–5.3
Advance Dev Mkts	♣	113	–1	140	106	–	129.9	13.0
Advance UK Trust	♣	129½	–2½	150	123	1.2	141.7	8.6
Advance Value Realisation		82½	....	100½	70½	–	80.5	–2.5
Pref		92½	....	100½	91½	–	–	–
Advent VCT	♣	73	+3½	100½	66	–	109.0	33.1
Advent 2 VCT	♣	70	–1	101½	70	19.9	87.8	20.2
Albany	♣	206½	+½	233	192	3.3	253.0	18.4
Alliance Tst	♣	3112½	+17½	3520	2887½	2.1	3512.1	11.4
AlternativeInv Strat	♣	118½	+¾	*136½	103½	–	111.7	–6.0
C		73	+½	7268½	66¾	–	67.6	–7.9
American Monthly	F	64xd	+¾	101½	56	13.4	69.3	7.7
Annuity	F	93xd	....	101½	92	16.1	–	–
Zero Dv Pf		103¼	–¼	111	99	–	106.7	3.3
American Opp	♣	106	....	123½	88½	–	121.9	13.0
Amerindo Internet	♣	28	+1¼	140¼	25½	–	35.2	20.4
Anglo & O'seas	♣	291	+6	390½	256	1.3	306.9	5.2
Archimedes Inc	†	122½	....	140½	114½	–	–	–
Cap		1022½	....	1090	895	–	1084.1	5.7
Artemis AIM VCT		95	....	110	94¾	–	95.0	0.0
Asian Technology	♣	20¼	+¼	43	19¾	–	25.3	19.8
Warrants		0¾	....	4	0¾	–	–	–
Asset Management Inv	♣sF	165½	....	200	139½	9.5	152.6	–8.4
Warrants		77	....	97½	41½	–	–	–
Zero Div Pref		146¼	....	147½	123½	–	133.5	–9.6

Figure 4.1 This is the way that investment trust share prices are shown in the *Financial Times*. The names of the trusts are listed in the left hand column. The club symbol indicates those trusts where a free annual report is available for those who call 020 8391 6000. The first column of figures shows the closing share price on the previous day, with the day's price change on the right. The next two columns show the closing high and low over the previous 52 weeks. Then comes the dividend yield in percentage terms. The penultimate column shows the net asset value (in pence per share). Lastly, the column shows the percentage premium (shown with a minus symbol) or discount at which the shares trade to net asset value.

Financial Times, July 2001

alters in line with market movements. New shares are not created when investors buy or sell. Thus, there are a fixed number of shares available for investors to buy and sell.

CLOSED-END AND OPEN-ENDED FUNDS

Investment trusts are also known as *closed-end* funds. The number of shares issued by the fund is set at the beginning. (Closed end in this context means limited.) New investors must buy shares from existing shareholders, rather than from the manager. Investment trusts trade at a price set by the market which may be above (a premium), below (a discount) or at the asset value of the fund (parity).

In contrast, unit trusts have no fixed capitalisation – i.e. the number of shares issued and outstanding. The quantity of shares changes depending on whether there are more purchases or more redemptions each business day. Unit trusts, which are known accordingly as *open-ended funds*, always trade at net asset value.

An investment trust has a great advantage over a unit trust if, say, share prices suddenly plunge. In this situation, a unit trust manager can find that he has to sell shares to meet the cash demands of his investors. The trust, therefore, must sell shares at the worst possible time, into a falling market. An investment trust manager, however, is not subject to this pressure. If shareholders in the trust sell their shares, this does not affect the value of the assets in the portfolio. The market value of the trust's outstanding shares change separated from the securities in the portfolio. The manager, therefore, does not have to sell part of his portfolio at all.

A closed-end structure can also be of help in a rising market. The chances are that, when the market is rising fast, a unit trust manager will receive lots of new cash from investors. He will have to throw that money into the market at a time when prices are high. Again, the investment trust manager can bide his time, waiting to invest any cash he may have at a more opportune time.

DISCOUNTS AND PREMIUMS

The fact that investment trusts do not always trade at asset value but at a discount or premium has restricted the growth of investment trusts. For a start, the way they work is confusing to the average investor. Second, it adds an extra level of risk. You could buy shares in a trust specialising in, say, UK equities hoping to benefit from a rise in the London stock market. If your hunch is right, the market goes up and so does the value of the assets in the investment trust. But the share price goes down, because the discount widens. Instead of having just one factor to worry about, you have two: the asset value and the level of the discount. However, it's easy to get too worked up over this issue. In fact, seasoned investors see these two factors as an advantage, especially if they have the patience to hold on to their shares for a long time.

If a trust is trading at a 20 per cent discount, then investors are getting 100p of assets for just 80p. Furthermore, there is always the chance that the discount will narrow. If that does happen, investors could enjoy a 'double whammy'. Say the assets in the portfolio rose by 20 per cent and the discount narrowed to 10 per cent. The share price would then rise from 80p to 108p (120p minus 10 per cent, or 12p). So, instead of a mere 20 per cent gain, they would have made a 35 per cent profit ((108p - 80p) ÷ 80p).

Why might the discount narrow? One reason would simply be a change in sentiment in the market that prompts more demand for the shares. Another might be that an outsider could mount a takeover bid and attempt to buy the trust at a price close to the asset value. The manager could also take action, either by buying back the trust shares in the market or by proposing to turn the fund into a unit trust (which always trades at asset value). Ideally, you should aim to buy when the discount is wide and sell when it is narrow (or if the share price goes to a premium).

NEW ISSUES

One consequence of the discount factor is that you should view new issues of investment trusts with scepticism. In the rest of the stock market, a lot of investors get very excited about new issues because of their potential to go to a big premium in early trading. But this is not likely to happen with a new investment trust for several reasons.

First of all, when a trust joins the stock market all it will have is cash. Investors should not pay a premium for that, any more than they should swap a £5 note for four pound coins. Second, investors will already be paying an effective premium for the cash in a new issue since the trust will deduct the costs of listing before it starts investing the proceeds in the market. If you invest 100p, only about 96p of that will go into the market. Third, there are lots of existing trusts trading at a discount. So unless the new issue has a particularly exciting angle, investors will probably feel there are more attractive opportunities elsewhere.

All the above reasons mean that most new issues drop to a discount to their opening price after launch. This makes it difficult to launch new issues. After all, why buy something at 100p, when it will probably fall to 90p in a couple of weeks? This is another factor that has restricted the size of the investment trust industry.

FEES

The discount factor can also obscure a great advantage of

investment trusts: they tend to be much cheaper than unit trusts. For a start, there is no initial charge, just the normal spread between bid and offer prices that all investors face when they buy any share. Annual charges can be (but aren't always) much lower as well. Unit trusts regularly charge 1–1.5 per cent a year. Some big investment trusts charge less than 0.5 per cent a year. That is a very cost-effective way of managing your money. This difference in charges should benefit investors in the long run. Although comparisons are difficult, investment trusts tend to outperform unit trusts in terms of asset growth.

The average UK general investment trust gained 264 per cent over the ten years to end 1999 while the average UK All Companies unit trust gained just 207.5 per cent. It has to be admitted that investment trusts will not always deliver a superior performance. The obvious examples are when investors buy at a time when trusts are on a narrow discount to their net asset value and sell when the discount is wide.

GEARING

One more big difference between unit and investment trusts should be mentioned. Investment trusts can borrow money to try to improve their performance. Suppose a trust has £100 million invested in shares. It decides to borrow another £10 million at an annual interest charge of 7 per cent. Assume also that the trust has 100 million shares, which trade at asset value, or £1 each. Over the next year the trust's investments rise by 20 per cent. Since it has £110 million invested, that means the gross assets of the fund have gone up to £132 million. Take off the £10 million in debt and the £700,000 in interest and the trust has £121.3 million. Its assets are up 21.3 per cent. Had it stuck with its original £100 million, the gain would have been just 20 per cent.

This sounds like good news. But, of course, there is a danger. If the trust's investments had fallen by 20 per cent, the borrowing, or *gearing* as it is called, would work against it. The gross assets would have fallen from £110 million to £88 million. Once the debt and the interest are removed, the amount of money left to shareholders would be just £77.3 million. The loss to investors would be 22.7 per cent. Had the fund not borrowed the money, they would have been just 20 per cent worse off.

So a trust's ability to borrow money adds to its riskiness. It is a power that needs to be used very carefully. Managers try only to borrow money when they think equities look cheap but they can get their timing wrong. Over the long run, however, share prices tend to go up, so gearing should improve performance.

EXPLAINING THE DISCOUNT

Why does the discount exist? There are several explanations. One is tax: if the trust were to be wound up and the assets sold off, shareholders could find their profits subject to capital gains tax. The second is charges: investment trust managers charge fees; they normally have a lengthy management contract in place. Again, if the trust were to be suddenly wound up and the assets sold, the manager would have to be paid off. But the most plausible answer is supply and demand.

When they were set up, investment trusts were designed for the private investor. But high tax rates after the Second World War meant that many private investors were forced out of the equity market. The institutions – insurance companies, pension funds and the like – ended up with big holdings of investment trust shares. That was fine for a while, but gradually many of those institutions decided that they could manage their equity portfolios on their own, or hire managers to do so at a lower cost. They were natural sellers of investment trust shares and there were not enough retail investors to take their place. In other words, there was a shortage of demand relative to supply; share prices fell in response and the discount widened.

Investment trusts have been restricted in their ability to tackle this problem. One difficulty is related to the law. As quoted companies, investment trusts are not allowed to advertise their own shares. The second difficulty is related to costs. Because investment trusts have low charges, they have little money to pay to advisers and brokers in the form of commission. Without that commission, the advisers have little incentive to recommend investment trusts – and so they often don't. Unit trusts, which are willing to pay 3 per cent upfront, get most of the business.

Now you may be wondering why, if financial advisers are supposed to be acting on your behalf, they recommend the more expensive option that suits them, instead of the cheaper option that suits you. Good question.

Investment trusts started to fight back in the 1980s, when Foreign & Colonial launched the first monthly savings scheme. Legally, it was decided that this approach did not break the law against advertising trust shares. Although savings schemes did not bring in huge sums right from the start, they did play a part in narrowing the discount. Savings schemes provide trusts with a steady drip-feed of money each month that can mop up the shares sold by institutional investors. The launch of *split capital trusts* (see later in the chapter) was another popular approach, allowing trusts to differentiate themselves from their unit-based rivals. Finally, the growing popularity of equity investing in the 1980s (thanks to lower tax rates and the success of the privatisation programme) enticed private investors back into the sector.

Investment trust savings schemes work on exactly the same principle as the unit trust schemes described in the last chapter. Investors put in a set amount a month with the aim of building up a lump sum over the long term. Like unit trust schemes, investment trust savings schemes benefit from pound cost averaging: you buy more shares when prices are low, fewer when they are high. But in this case, investors get a double benefit, because of the discount effect. They buy more shares when the discount is wide and fewer when the discount is narrow.

Investment trusts are also a potential investment for an individual savings account (ISA). Most fund managers advertise their own plans but you can pick and choose your own investment trusts if you have a self-select ISA. Investments in an ISA are free of capital gains tax and there is also a tax break on dividend income until 2004.

TYPES OF INVESTMENT TRUSTS

Just like unit trusts, investment trusts come in all shapes and sizes. So before you invest in the sector, you should decide which sort of trust you want.

The international generalists These trusts are the forefathers of the entire sector. They include giants such as Foreign & Colonial, and Alliance, and they invest in shares across the globe, wherever they feel the opportunities are best. For many investors these are likely to be the ideal core holding – the type of investment you lock away in your bottom drawer.

UK trusts These trusts invest in the UK equity market. There are few of these trusts left (just twenty-six in early 2001), thanks to the superior marketing skills of unit trusts and the lack of demand from institutional investors.

Income trusts These trusts invest in shares with a higher

dividend yield with the aim of paying a higher income to investors. Capital growth will probably not be as good as on a general trust.

Emerging market trusts These trusts invest in the stock markets of developing countries in South-East Asia and Latin America. The trusts were very popular in the early 1990s, but fell heavily after the Mexican peso crisis of late 1994 and the South-East Asian crisis of 1997–8.

Individual country trusts These invest in the shares quoted on one particular stock market, such as Korea or Hong Kong. These are highly specialised areas, and private investors should only consider them after they have built up substantial UK and broad-based global portfolios.

Smaller company trusts These trusts invest in smaller quoted companies, an approach that has worked very well in the past but not so well in the 1990s.

Venture capital trusts These trusts invest in small, unquoted companies that they hope to float on the stock market or to sell to a bigger company. The risks are high, but so are the potential rewards. In fact, the biggest trust of all – 3i (it stands for Investors in Industry) – is in this sector.

Property trusts There were only three of these trusts in early 2001. They specialise in investing in the shares of property companies. Property trusts have tended to be fairly safe but not very exciting investments but may attract those who believe that property prices are due for a substantial increase.

SPLIT CAPITAL INVESTMENT TRUSTS

The fact that investment trusts are stock market companies gives them a lot more scope to be inventive about their structure. For example, conventional investors get both the dividends and the capital growth a company provides. But why should that be? After all, some investors want the income while others are more interested in capital growth. *Split capital investment trusts* are designed to take advantage of different investment goals. To do this, the managers create more than one class of share. There are many different structures but the three most common share types are income, capital and zero dividend shares.

Income shares As the name suggests, these receive all the income that the trust receives in the form of dividend or interest payments. They usually offer a high yield, much higher than an ordinary share or even a building society investment. But this income is likely to come at the expense of capital growth. In some cases, an income share might be issued at 100p but will only be repaid at 1p. So the high income in those cases is an illusion; you could achieve a similar effect by selling, say, 10 per cent of your investments every year.

Capital shares These receive all the growth of the trust (but no income). So if the fund performs very well, the value of these shares will rise very sharply. Again there is a risk attached. To please the income shareholders, the trust manager may have to invest in some very high yielding shares. Those shares may not grow much in value. So the capital shares may not get much growth to enjoy. And if the trust performs badly, capital shareholders could lose most, or all, of their money.

Zero dividend preference shares These receive no income, but enjoy a set rate of capital growth. For example, the shares might be issued at 100p with a promise of being repaid at 200p in ten years' time. So these tend to be safe and steady investments. They are not 100 per cent secure, however, since the trust's assets may not grow sufficiently to meet the repayment value. Note also that if a trust has capital and zero dividend preference shares, the capital shareholders are second in the queue if the company is liquidated, since preference shareholders always have first claim on a company's assets.

Warrant Warrants are not used purely in split capital trust structures. Many conventional trusts have them as well. They give the investor the chance to buy more shares in the trust at a set price. If the share price is above this price, it may be worth exercising the warrants. If the share price is below the set price, it is definitely not worth doing so.

Split capital investment trust shares can be complicated and new investors should only really get into this sector after taking professional advice. Their main attractions are related to tax and financial planning. Zero dividend shares could be bought as part of a plan for meeting a future commitment, such as a wedding or school fees. Investors would have the security of knowing they should get the right money at the right time. And if they have not used up their annual capital gains tax allowance, the profits might be tax-free.

The popularity of split capital issues has waxed and waned; recently they have made a comeback after a fallow period in the mid 1990s. One problem is that it is difficult to run a trust with the aim of pleasing so many different classes of shareholders – some who want capital and some who want income. This has sometimes led to disappointment for some investors.

CHAPTER FIVE

INTERNATIONAL INVESTING

I n 1997, when I was travelling around Britain filming my television show, *Investing for All with Alvin Hall*, I spent a large part of every day with a cellphone pressed to my ear. At the time, Americans were behind the UK in cellphone technology. I became intrigued by this great new (and supposedly brain-addling) device, and had a hunch that it would soon become a big hit in the US. I knew virtually nothing about cellphones, however. So I went into a London phone store and began asking questions. I was looking for the easiest to use, best-looking, best-valued cellphone on the market, I explained. And then I asked for the salespeople's recommendations. In this way, I discovered Nokia, a company I'd never heard of before. I went home, logged on to the Internet, and conducted further research. The next day, I (an American) called up my stockbroker (in London) and bought as many shares in Nokia (a Finnish company) as I could afford. It turned out to be one of my best picks ever.

As I look to the UK, Europe or Asia for my overseas investments, you might consider the US, the largest equities market in the world, for investment opportunities. As impressive as British companies may be, the truth is that only a fraction of the world's largest companies are traded on the London Stock Exchange. Today many Britons work for, or use the products of, overseas corporations. You have undoubtedly heard about the fortunes made in the late 1990s by investors in non-British shares, such as Cisco Systems, Oracle or Dell Computer – if they sold before the technology meltdown which began in 2000, when the prices of all these shares collapsed. So it is natural that you may be tempted to put some of your savings into overseas shares. Indeed, as more and more people try their hand at investing out of their home markets, it is becoming easier and cheaper to do so.

One approach to venturing overseas is by investing in one of the many UK companies that have worldwide operations. It has been estimated that around 50 per cent of the sales of the FTSE 100 companies come from outside the UK. Take Vodafone, for example: you may think of it as simply a UK mobile phone group, but thanks to some big acquisitions in recent years it is truly a global group now, with mobile operations in the US (through Airtouch) and across Europe (through Mannesmann). The oil giants BP and Shell are clearly far more dependent on the price of oil, set internationally and priced in dollars, than they are on the UK economy. So you can get quite a good spread of international exposure while keeping your investments in the London market.

It is also worth noting that there are some overseas companies that have a listing in London as well as on their own exchange. Large companies often do this (just as some UK companies have listings in New York or Tokyo) so they can appeal to a wider range of investors. You can find lists of such companies in the share price pages of the *Financial Times* under the headings Americans, Canadians and South Africans. Among the companies featured there are AT&T,

Ford, Gillette and Quaker Oats. Further companies can be found in their individual sectors: for example Ericsson and Motorola, the mobile phone manufacturers, are grouped under Information Technology Hardware. You can buy these shares through a stockbroker and pay standard commission rates.

Nevertheless, there are lots of exciting companies that are not listed in London, particularly in the technology sector. And overseas stock markets can sometimes perform a lot better than the London market: Tokyo in the 1980s and Wall Street in the 1990s are two prime examples.

It is likely that, in five or ten years' time, investing in overseas companies will be as commonplace as going on overseas holidays.

Stock markets are gradually becoming more international. A planned merger between the London and Frankfurt stock exchanges in 2000 fell through but it seems likely that, at some point, the London exchange will link up with overseas markets. Eventually the world's stock markets may all integrate into one, globe-spanning, computer-based market in which companies from Andorra to Zambia are all traded twenty-four hours a day, 365 days a year.

THE DIFFICULTIES OF OVERSEAS INVESTING
Regardless of how the worldwide market changes, several underlying problems will always confront investors.

First, there is the problem of *currency risk*. Overseas shares will be denominated in, and pay dividends in, a currency that is not sterling. This means UK investors are exposed to the risk that the currency will fall in value against the pound. You could pick the right stock but make no money at all in sterling terms, because the overseas currency fell against the pound. Also a broker will normally require you to hold funds in a foreign currency denominated account (usually dollars or euros) before you can trade. So you could lose money on currency movements even without buying any shares at all.

Of course, you could make money if the pound falls in value against the currency in which either your shares, or your brokerage account, is denominated. And, alas, for much of the past 100 years, the pound has been in a declining trend against other major currencies.

One long-term result of any European stock exchange merger could be that all UK stocks will be quoted in euros. This would not be popular with UK investors but it would mean that, in currency risk terms, there would be nothing to choose between UK and European stocks. Another possibility is that the UK will eventually sign up for the single European currency, although opinion polls indicate that the majority of the population is opposed to the idea.

The second problem is that of *cost*. Dealing in overseas shares can be more expensive. Some brokers will charge a higher commission and there may be custody costs in terms of holding share certificates. Receiving dividends in a foreign currency will either require you to set up a bank account in that currency or to incur foreign exchange costs every time a dividend is paid. The broker may also make a charge for currency conversions when you make sterling payments into your account.

The cost position is improving, however. In many other stock markets, stamp duty (a tax on share purchases) is either charged at a lower rate than in the UK, or is non-existent. Bid-offer spreads can be lower in the US market than they are in the UK. US brokerage firms are now offering online services in the UK, where the rates charged to buy US shares are no more expensive than those available to US investors.

However, they are not designed for very small investors. At the time of writing, both Charles Schwab & Co. and CSFB*direct* require a minimum deposit of $10,000 (£7,000 at the time of writing) to start trading in US shares.

INVESTING DIRECTLY OVERSEAS

There are two ways of getting involved in overseas shares. It is more appropriate for the small investor – one with only a few hundred or a thousand pounds to invest – to use a unit trust or an investment trust (see Chapters 3 and 4). These can give you a broad spread of international companies without the administrative hassle and extra cost of share ownership overseas.

If you are determined to buy overseas shares directly, the first step is to look at the blue chips in Europe and the US. (So-called blue chips, named after the most valuable poker chips, refer to the shares of large, profitable, well-known public companies.) In Europe, you could look at the components of the Dow Jones Stoxx index (which has fifty components) or the FTSE Eurotop 300 (which includes both UK and European companies). The *Financial Times* lists the Eurotop 300 components by sector every day. For smaller companies and fast-growing technology groups, there is also the Euro-NM, an alliance of five bourses in Paris, Frankfurt, Amsterdam, Milan and Brussels, and NASDAQ Europe, a European version of the US NASDAQ market.

In the US the first port of call is the Dow Jones Industrial Average (DJIA), which includes thirty of the country's leading corporate names. A wider selection can be found in the Standard & Poors 500 index. The NASDAQ Composite index includes the leading US technology stocks.

Individual countries also have their blue-chip indices. In Germany there is the Dax, which contains thirty leading stocks. In France there is the CAC40 index, which, as the name suggests, contains forty large companies. Japan has the Nikkei 225 average and so on.

One needs to be aware, however, that not all of these indices operate like the FTSE 100. The companies in the DJIA are not the thirty largest in the US but a selection of stocks that the editors of *The Wall Street Journal* think reflect the overall market. The Nikkei 225 in Japan contains some old industrial stocks that are very small in size.

Finding the name is, in any case, only a start. You will obviously need to find some financial details about the group concerned. Many companies now have their own websites, packed with information about the company's activities and its latest financial data. This is obviously not an unbiased source but it should at least give you a clear idea of what the company does.

There are some independent sites that give access to European-wide information. One such site is *www.european investor.com*, which provides market news, broker ratings, information guides and much besides. There is an excellent company database at *www.wisi.com*, from the US investment management group Wright Information Services. Just enter the name of the company you are interested in, and if it is on the database you will get a company description, financial information, key valuation numbers and Wright's own assessment of the company's worth.

Newspapers such as the *Financial Times* and *The Wall Street Journal Europe* also bring daily reports on international company news such as results, share price movements, new issues and mergers and acquisitions. And there are many good articles in publications such as *Fortune*, *Forbes*, *BusinessWeek* and *Barron's*.

Companies in different countries report figures in different ways. In Germany, for example, the accounting process is linked to the taxation process. That gives German companies an incentive to report lower profits, because they will then pay less tax. Different countries have different approaches to issues such as depreciation of assets or acquisitions.

WHAT PERCENTAGE OF YOUR PORTFOLIO SHOULD BE OVERSEAS?

There is no magical answer to this question, but there are two approaches to take: the strategic and the tactical.

The *strategic* approach is to work out what your exposure to overseas economic developments will be in the long run. While this may seem like an odd assignment, it isn't really. We all save for a reason, and that reason is to have money to spend at a later date – on university fees, a daughter's wedding, or on our own retirement. It may be, for example, that you would like to retire to a holiday home in Spain. In that case, a lot of your long-term spending will be in euros, not pounds, so a higher exposure to overseas equities is appropriate. If, however, you plan to retire to Brighton and spend your money on beer and chips, your overseas exposure should be limited. As a guide, pension funds, which have to meet the income expectations of future retirees, tend to have around 20–25 per cent of their portfolios in overseas equities.

The *tactical* approach depends on whether you think that the UK will do better or worse than other markets in the short term (over the next few years). As I have said before, timing the market is difficult. But there clearly have been times when other markets have performed substantially better than the London stock market in sterling terms. For example, in the late 1990s the UK stock market stagnated while Wall Street and European bourses surged.

However, the exposure to different countries may not be as important as the exposure to different sectors. There are no quoted automobile manufacturers in the UK any more. If you believe in the auto sector, you have to buy overseas stocks. A lot of the world's leading technology companies, such as Microsoft, Intel and SAP are all based overseas. And mobile phone manufacturers (as distinct from the mobile phone operators) such as Nokia and Motorola are all based outside the UK.

DEALING IN OVERSEAS SHARES

You first need to find a broker who specialises in overseas shares. The Association of Private Client Investment Managers and Stockbrokers (APCIMS) is a good resource: its address is 112 Middlesex Street, London E1 7HY. And the Internet provides some useful assessments of broker services at sites such as *www.iii.co.uk, www.moneyworld.co.uk* and *www.fool.co.uk*.

It is worth shopping around, particularly if you are interested in US shares, now that US stockbrokers offer services in London. Check for the following things:

- Are commissions higher in the UK than in the US on US stocks?
- Are you required to open a foreign currency account?
- Are there extra administrative charges?
- Can you receive annual reports from the company concerned?

If you want to trade in US stocks, you should complete a W-8 form from the US Internal Revenue Service. This gives you the status of a 'non-resident alien' under the US tax code and means you are not taxed in the US on any profits you make. Alas, you will still be liable to pay capital gains tax in the UK on any profits and income tax on any dividends received (as you will on shares from other countries).

If you want to use a European broker to trade, life can be a little more difficult. German brokers require customers to have a German bank account when they trade and that, in turn, requires German residency or citizenship. Life is rather easier with brokers in Switzerland or Luxembourg but you will still need to send your broker a copy of your passport and a letter from your bank.

One favourable UK tax change is that overseas stocks can now be held within an individual savings account (ISA). This means that any capital gains will be tax-free. Under the old personal equity plan (PEP) rules, this advantage was only available to investors in European Union stocks.

PRICING

Share prices can differ quite sharply from one country to another. This has nothing to do with whether share prices are cheap or expensive: it is normally a matter of national custom. In European countries, for example, leading company shares may sell for many hundreds of euros. All this means is that if you invest £2,000 or £3,000 you may only get a handful of shares. In the US share prices tend to be a bit higher than those in the UK – say $20 to $100 – but not as high as those in Europe.

In both cases, this makes no difference whatsoever. What really does make a difference are the assets and earnings that back up those shares. Because share prices are higher and the number of shares in issue fewer, the average earnings per share of a European or US company will be higher than the average earnings per share of a UK company. The same amount of earnings is spread among a smaller number of shares.

Buying overseas shares is not for every first-time investor. In general, it is better to find your feet in the UK market first; or, if you feel compelled to invest abroad, start with a unit trust or investment trust that buys overseas shares. But as you gain experience, it is certainly worth looking at opportunities in other markets.

CHAPTER SIX

FUNDAMENTAL ANALYSIS: EVALUATING A COMPANY FROM THE INSIDE

D ECIDING which shares to buy can be interesting and fun, but it also requires a certain amount of 'hard chair time', as my grandmother used to say. How, for example, do you assess whether a share is cheap or expensive? That's what used to be called the $64,000 question, but now thanks to inflation and Chris Tarrant it should probably be called the £1 million query. Actually, it's the kind of question that comes up in the process of *fundamental analysis*: the evaluation of a company through scrutiny of its balance sheet, income statement, management, marketing and sales, and research and development.

It took me a long time and a lot of hard work to understand fundamental analysis, but it was unquestionably time well spent. I read the business section of newspapers and books on things like price-earnings (P/E) ratios, and peppered everyone I knew in finance with questions. What I learned was that in picking shares you must research the facts and numbers that describe the health of a business; otherwise, you will be taking uninformed – and unnecessary – risks with your money.

Analysis is a subject that is at once difficult and easy to use. It is difficult to pick shares because millions of investors, many with years of experience, are trying to do the same thing. But it is easy to pick shares if you can afford to build a diversified portfolio. A broad spread of shares usually grows with time and surpasses the returns available from a building society account. If you spread your money in the market wisely, then you should do well over the long term.

One friend likens effective analysis to surgery: your challenge is to know the body's (or company's) major systems well, go in with a plan, get your hands dirty, try to work quickly and make intelligent choices. You don't have to know every single thing about a company, but you do need to know enough about the major aspects of its operations to make an informed decision.

Eventually, analysis becomes like sex: it has to be a hands-on experience for it to make any sense. This chapter aims to teach you the fundamentals of analysis and get you started. It isn't necessary to apply all these points to every investment you make. Choose the three or four approaches that you like best, and use them until you have a degree of mastery. Then, as you gain experience, add new elements to your analytical repertoire.

VALUING SHARES

As an investor, you are looking to put your money into a company that has performed well over the long term or is rapidly improving its market share. Remember that a share is a share of a company's assets, profits and dividends. But how do you research and monitor these key measurements?

Big financial firms in the City employ teams of analysts to forecast the future of company profits and to recommend shares that they think will rise in price. That information is valuable, but unfortunately analysts don't pass their forecasts directly on to private investors. They concentrate on the big fund management groups whose trades bring in the bulk of their income.

If you hire an advisory broker (see Chapter 10), you can access some of this research, but that requires you pay high commissions when you deal. And you can learn some of what the analysts are forecasting through publications such as *Company Refs* and websites such as *www.iii.co.uk* (Interactive Investor International).

The key question for investors is: how much are a company's earnings per share expected to rise or fall? And have analysts' forecasts been increasing or decreasing recently? The share price of a company normally does well when forecasts are rising, and this is a trend that can last for some time. Analysts don't change their forecasts all at once, but if one has upgraded – or downgraded – others are likely to follow suit.

You should look for companies that expect to grow their earnings at a rate faster than that of the rest of the market. Of course, it isn't easy to know what the overall market is expected to achieve. A good rule of thumb is that corporate earnings will rise in line with the economy, and the economy is likely to rise by 5–6 per cent a year in nominal terms. Any company whose earnings are growing faster than that – particularly if growth is in double digits – is performing well.

It is much more important to pay attention to the forecast numbers than to the analysts' recommendation for the stock. Analysts have mixed allegiances, and must choose their words carefully. Likewise, you should listen to them selectively, or at least sceptically. Analysts generally make positive noises about shares, issuing recommendations such as 'buy' or 'market outperform'. But don't forget that their employers are trying to persuade corporations to use them to make acquisitions, issue new shares or raise debt. It is difficult to win the heart of an executive when your firm's analyst is telling investors to sell the executive's stock. So that kind of blunt recommendation rarely happens. Furthermore, if an analyst is negative on a stock, then the company may cut off all communication with him: when there is big news to report, the company will not return the analyst's calls and he will find it difficult to do his job.

So analysts are forced to resort to code. The worst they will say about a stock is that it is a 'hold' or a 'market underperformer'. More often than not, this is bad news. Their institutional clients know that the real meaning is 'sell', but private investors may not always be clued in.

Investors should also be cautious about newspaper 'tips'. Sometimes a tip is reported in good faith by a journalist, but is based on a faulty source. Sometimes a tip is purely a journalist's opinion. While reporters may know more than you about a particular company, you should ask yourself: 'If this journalist is so smart, how come he is slaving away over a computer screen instead of lounging on his yacht off Bermuda?'

The same principle applies to tips on Internet bulletin boards, where you have literally no idea where the information is coming from. It could be coming from a crank who is guessing, or fabricating information. Or it could be coming from someone more sinister: an investor who already owns the shares and wants to force the price up so he can sell them at a profit, a practice known as 'pumping and dumping'.

Alas, there is no one perfect way of valuing shares. If it is obvious that a share has been undervalued, then investors rush to buy it, the price goes up, and it is no longer cheap.

SIGNS OF SUCCESS

Successful companies come in many shapes and sizes, and it is hard to make sweeping generalisations about them. But here are a few classic types to look out for.

The better mousetrap company 'If you build a better mouse-trap, the world will beat a path to your door,' the old saying goes. Occasionally a company will appear with a better mousetrap – a product so good that its success is virtually guaranteed. A great example of this is Glaxo, the pharmaceutical group, which was phenomenally successful in the 1980s because of its anti-ulcer drug Zantac. The drugs industry is often the place where such innovations occur; the industry has a crucial advantage in that its products are protected by patent and new drugs face severe regulatory tests before they can be used. This protects drugs companies from competition and allows them to earn high margins.

Technology is another field where 'better mousetraps' can be found. A Cambridge-based company, ARM Holdings, has leaped into the FTSE 100 index after only two years on the stock market. Its chip designs are so good that they will be used in the next generation of mobile phones, and potentially in thousands of other devices. Another UK technological success, NXT, has designed a new flat-screen loudspeaker that dramatically cuts the weight of household devices such as TVs.

The franchise These companies have an established brand-name business that consumers will turn to again and again. For a long time, Marks and Spencer was perceived to have this quality because of its ability to deliver excellent food and clothing at a competitive price. Sadly, M&S lost this reputation in the late 1990s and its share price duly suffered.

The key advantage of a franchise is that it protects the company against competition. It is hardly worth a rival attempting to attack the business. A good US example is Gillette, which has an overwhelmingly strong position in the razor market. Consumers use its products every day and its name is recognised worldwide. But the best example of all is Microsoft: Bill Gates's software company dominates the industry so that most of the world's computers use its systems.

The industry consolidator Sometimes a business can prosper even in an industry that is not growing fast. One approach is to consolidate the business via acquisitions. That way, the company can achieve economies of scale and reduce cut-throat competition. General Motors achieved this feat back in the early days of the US car industry, and media companies such as AOL/Time-Warner and Seagram/Vivendi are in the process of consolidating now.

The well-managed company Some businesses simply have better managers and/or a better strategy than their rivals. A good example of this is Wal-Mart, the American discount store chain founded by Sam Walton. Terrific attention to detail, cost control and the most efficient distribution system in the world allow Wal-Mart to offer consumers a wide range of goods at rock-bottom prices. It has simply blown its competition away.

In the UK, Lloyds TSB became the most successful bank by making the management decision to concentrate on the domestic retail market instead of pursuing the dream of becoming a global investment bank. Two of its rivals, Barclays and NatWest, were forced to pull out of investment banking, and NatWest was taken over by Royal Bank of Scotland, while a third, Midland, was sold to Hong Kong and Shanghai Banking Corporation.

The fast-growing industry There is an old saying that 'a rising tide lifts all boats'. Some industries are growing so strongly that almost all the operators in it will be carried along for the ride. A recent example of this is the mobile phone industry, which made investors in Vodafone, Orange, Cable & Wireless (which owned One-2-One) and Securicor (which owned half of Cellnet) substantial profits in the 1990s.

SIGNS OF DISTRESS

The types of company that are unlikely to be good investments include:

The poorly managed company Has the company recently issued a couple of profit warnings that have forced the share price to tumble? Does it have a reputation for letting down its investors? Such companies are to be avoided. Occasionally new managers can be appointed and turn a company round, bringing investors healthy profits. But normally when a company – even a large, well-established one such as Xerox or Kodak – has a record of disappointments, investors are very unlikely to forgive the management or purchase the stock.

The company with a bad reputation There is no sure-fire way of avoiding fraudulent companies, but it is safer to avoid companies with a dubious reputation. Factors to watch for include: past investigations by the Department of Trade and Industry; a labyrinthine corporate structure, with lots of different holding companies and subsidiaries, where the management frequently shifts assets between the businesses; high debt levels; a board where one executive clearly wields all the power and there are no checks and balances.

A classic example of this was Mirror Group Newspapers, run by the late Robert Maxwell.

The commodity goods producer These are companies that produce goods that have no added value or distinguishing characteristics, such as manufacturers of bulk chemicals. Such companies have lots of rivals who produce the same product to the same standard, and their only way to compete is on price. Their margins tend to be low, and the business is vulnerable to fight-to-the-death price wars. This can be very bad news, indeed, for an unwary investor.

The above factors will give you an indication as to whether or not a company is worth investing in. The next question is can you invest in that business at a good price?

SHARE PRICE

The first thing to say about picking shares is that the actual share price *alone* tells you nothing. This can be a psychological barrier for some investors, but it's logical if you think it through. After all, whether a share is priced at 3p or £10 tells you nothing about the health and prospects of a company, if that's all you know about it. Say there were only four shares in Vodafone: one of those shares would be a bargain at a billion pounds, since the company is valued at tens of billions. Similarly, shares in a bankrupt company would be expensive at 1p, because the underlying business is worth nothing. What matters to investors is the level of company profits, assets and dividends that the share gives you.

The actual share price is usually a combination of historical accident and whim. Some companies join the market at 50p, others at £4. A company may split its shares (see Chapter 2) to lower the price, or consolidate the shares to make the price higher. In neither case, however, is the underlying value of the company affected.

Some investors are obsessed with share price, and favour *penny shares*, so-called because their price is less than £1. Penny shares tend to be associated with small companies, and statistics show that shares in smaller companies tend to outperform shares in larger ones over the long term. But this increased performance comes at an increased risk. Small companies are often dependent on one product or a few customers, and are thus vulnerable to sudden changes in the market.

Investors who like penny shares reason that 'if the shares are 50p, the upside is enormous; they could go up to £5, and I would increase my money tenfold.' But this is somewhat self-deluding. There is nothing to stop a £5 share price going to £50, or a £50 share price going to £500. Indeed, in the US a single share in Warren Buffett's company, Berkshire Hathaway, has been valued at $70,000 (currently some £50,000).

What really matters is not share price, but whether a company is healthy and competitive and can show a rapid growth in profits and assets.

Say you have two companies, one with 100 million shares and the other with 1 million shares, and each is worth £10 million. The first company's shares trade at 10p, the second at £10. If both companies' value increased by 10 per cent, to £11 million, then the value of each share would rise by 10 per cent as well – to 11p and £11 respectively. Shareholders in either company would have done equally as well.

The other illusion associated with penny shares is that you get 'more shares for your money'. Some people prefer getting, say, 2,000 shares at 50p each rather than 100 shares at £10 each. But the bottom line is that both have invested £1,000. Would you rather have two slices of a pizza cut into eighths, or one slice of the same pizza cut into quarters? At the end of the day, they are the same.

Often you will find that the spread between the buying and selling price for penny shares is very high. Say you see a share that is quoted in the paper as being priced at 3p. It may be that this price is between a bid of 2.5p and an offer of 3.5p. In other words if you buy the shares, you will pay 3.5p. If you immediately wanted to sell the shares, you would only receive the bid price of 2.5p. The bid price will thus have to rise from 2.5p to 3.5p, a difference of 40 per cent, just for you to break even – and that doesn't allow for dealing costs, such as broker's commission and stamp duty.

So, if looking at the share price alone is the wrong answer, what is the right one? There is no perfect solution, but a starting point is to look at the four following measures: the price-earnings ratio, net asset value, dividend yield and cash flow measures.

PRICE-EARNINGS RATIO (P/E)

The P/E is a shorthand method for comparing a company's profits with its share price. The first step is to work out which part of a company's profits go to ordinary shareholders alone. Alas, companies have a lot of other costs to meet before the shareholders receive their due: interest payments go to banks, bondholders and other creditors; tax goes to the government; preference dividends go to preference shareholders. What is left after all these deductions is known as shareholders' earnings. This figure is dubbed 'the bottom line'. You may have heard the phrase 'this will go straight through to the bottom line.' This means that shareholders will get all the benefit of some development.

But even calculating the shareholders' earnings only gets us part of the way. Say a company has earnings of £50 million a year – how does that relate to a share price of 200p?

The next step is to divide the earnings by the number of shares in issue. Suppose our company with £50 million of earnings had 500 million shares. That is equivalent to *earnings per share* of 10p. Of course the company does not pay out 10p per share to every shareholder. It retains some (usually most) of the earnings to help expand the business. But in theory, 10p is each shareholder's entitlement.

The final step is to divide the share price by the earnings per share. In this case, we divide 200p by 10. That gives a figure – the P/E ratio – of 20.

What on earth does this mean? One way of looking at it is to imagine that the company did indeed pay out all its earnings to shareholders. Thus if you bought the shares at the prevailing price, and the earnings stayed the same, it would take twenty years before you got your money back. So a straightforward approach would be to assume that shares trading on a low P/E ratio are cheap because it will take fewer years for you to get your money back. Alas, it is not quite as simple as that.

Company profits are not stable. In most cases they are expected to grow, sometimes substantially, in future years. The higher that growth, the more investors should be willing to pay for the shares.

Let's take two companies, Go-Ahead Co. and Stick-in-the-Mud, Inc. Their figures are set out below:

	G-A	S-I-T-M
EARNINGS	£10M	£10M
SHARES	100M	100M
EARNINGS PER SHARE	10P	10P
SHARE PRICE	200P	100P
P/E RATIO	20	10

Which is the better deal? At first glance, it would seem to be the shares in Stick-in-the Mud on a P/E of just 10. But those figures relate to the past; investors are looking to the future.

In a year's time, Go-Ahead's earnings are expected to rise to 16p per share, while Stick-in-the-Mud's are expected to fall to 8p. Using those figures we can calculate what is called the *prospective P/E ratio*. Go-Ahead's ratio has fallen from 20 to 12.5, while Stick-in-the-Mud's ratio has risen to the same level. Now which is the better deal? If we then assume that Go-Ahead's earnings will keep rising rapidly, it is no contest.

So companies that trade on a high historic P/E will often be those where investors expect earnings to rise very rapidly in the future. And companies on low P/Es are expected to have earnings that grow slowly, stagnate or even decline.

High P/E shares tend to come from high-growth industries such as software, mobile telecoms or pharmaceuticals. Companies with low P/Es tend to be in slow-growing businesses such as paper and packaging or water. So when you look at a company's P/E, check to see how it compares with that of its sector as well as the market. Say the market is trading on a P/E of 20 and you spot an engineering company that sells for 18 times earnings: you might think that the shares are cheap. But if you look more closely, you might find that the average engineering company can only command a P/E of 16; your chosen stock is actually expensive relative to its peers.

The trick is to spot where the markets have got it wrong. There may be some stocks trading on a low P/E where the markets have overreacted to bad news and have not spotted that a recovery is round the corner. There may be stocks on a very high P/E where the markets have underestimated the potential for profit growth.

Each approach has its dangers. It is easy to buy a share on a low P/E on the grounds that it is 'cheap', only to find that the markets had very good reasons for giving it a low rating. Some businesses are in long-term decline – profits will keep on falling for years and no amount of management or strategic changes will turn them round. The 'cheap' stock just keeps getting cheaper.

The danger of buying high P/E shares is that it is possible to pay too much, even for a good company. Sometimes investor enthusiasm can bid up shares to ridiculous levels. Owning high P/E stocks exposes investors to the dangers of a 'double whammy'. When the company disappoints on earnings, its rating (the P/E) will fall as well.

Take Wondertech, a technology stock that is expected to grow its earnings from 40p a share this year to 60p next year. Because of its great growth prospects, Wondertech's shares are trading on a P/E of 40 times next year's earnings or (40 × 60p) £24. Suddenly, Wondertech announces that it's not going to make 60p per share next year but 50p. That is still a pretty good annual growth rate of 25 per cent. Nevertheless, investors are very disappointed and reckon Wondertech is now only worth a P/E rating of 30 times expected earnings. Thirty times 50p is just £15. So the shares fall by 37.5 per cent. So when you buy a high P/E stock, you need to be pretty confident it can maintain its growth rate. If it doesn't, you could be in for trouble.

The price-earnings ratio has been used as a valuation method for many years but it has its flaws. One is in the measurement of earnings. You might think that it is easy to measure a company's profits: see how much it has in the bank at the start of the financial year, and compare that to how much it has at the end of the year: the difference is the profit (or loss).

In reality, it's not as simple as that. Costs are charged and revenues booked even when no cash has changed hands. Take a company with plant and equipment, for example. That plant and equipment will eventually wear out and have to be replaced. One approach would simply be to record those costs as and when they occur. But this would result in very volatile profits and might not give a 'true and fair' picture of the business. Investors might be misled in thinking profits were high, only to find that profits slump the following year when half the machinery is replaced.

To avoid this problem, accountants make a *depreciation* charge. They assume that equipment will wear out over five, ten or twenty years, and they deduct a suitable proportion from profits each year to cover the eventual replacement cost. This smooths out the process. Similarly a company operating a long-term contract could decide to account for its money only when it gets paid, at the end. But an alternative approach is to spread out the payments over the lifetime of the contract.

Those are just two examples. The key point is that it is possible to manipulate the level of reported earnings (and the normal approach, of course, is to overestimate).

One much-used trick is for a company with a high price-earnings ratio to buy another with a low ratio. Let's return to Go-Ahead and Stick-in-the Mud. Go-Ahead has £10 million of earnings, 100 million shares and earnings per share of 10p. So does Stick-in-the-Mud. But Go-Ahead's share price is 200p (a P/E of 20) and Stick's share price is 100p (a P/E of 10). Assume that Go-Ahead decides to bid for Stick. It offers three of its shares for every five in Stick. Three Go-Ahead shares are worth 600p so that equates to a price per Stick share of 120p, 20 per cent above the market. Stick investors rush to accept and the offer is successful.

So now we have a new company, GoStick. It has £20 million of earnings. It has the original 100 million Go-Ahead shares plus another 60 million issued to buy Stick (three-fifths of 100 million). Thus it has 160 million shares in total. GoStick's earnings per share are £20 million divided by 160 million, or 12.5p. So for GoAhead shareholders, their earnings per share have increased from 10p to 12.5p, a rise of 25 per cent. This is without the company actually doing anything, such as rationalising offices, eliminating duplicate services and the like.

Companies that are highly acquisitive can see their earnings per share grow rapidly because of the above effect. But that can be an illusion; the underlying businesses may not be doing well at all.

Another difficulty with price-earnings ratios has cropped up in the last few years: what happens if the company isn't making any profits at all? Many technology companies have joined the market (particularly in the Internet area) while still making a loss. Obviously the companies have some value, because of their potential for future profits. But the price-earnings ratio is not much of a guide.

NET ASSET VALUE

A share also gives investors a stake in a company's assets. So an alternative approach is to link the share price to some measure of those assets, of which the standard approach is the net asset value.

The first step is to value all the assets. The management might get a chartered surveyor to assess the value of the properties the company owns. It might value the plant and machinery at cost, minus the depreciation charge (see above). Then there will be unsold stock, cash in the bank, shares in other companies and so on. When all that is done, the management must deduct a figure to allow for its debts. This is because debtors have a prior claim over its assets if it goes bust; the shareholders only get what is left when they have taken their cash.

The remaining figure is the net asset value. Dividing it by the number of shares in issue brings one to the net asset value per share.

Acme Property has a share price of 170p, but its net asset

value is 200p per share. So you might assume that the shares are attractive. After all, an investor could buy up all the shares, sell all the assets and come out with a profit. But Acme could face capital gains tax if it sold its properties. And the stated net asset value might not equal the amount Acme would receive if it tried to sell all its properties on the open market. In fact, property companies quite regularly trade at a discount to net assets.

When shares trade at a discount to net asset value, it may well be a sign that: (1) there would be a lot of difficulty in realising the full value of the assets; or (2) the market simply does not believe the asset value stated on the company's balance sheet.

Most companies trade at a premium to their asset value. Does this mean they are expensive? Not necessarily. All the measures I mentioned above concern what are called *tangible assets* – literally things you can touch, such as buildings and machinery.

But a lot of businesses make their money from *intangible assets*. They are just as real as tangible assets, but they don't get measured on a balance sheet. Take Coca-Cola. The company has a great brand name that is recognised all over the world. That obviously has a value that works in the company's favour. But it's not something you can touch or measure sufficiently well to put a balance sheet value on it. Or look at software: you can't touch it, but it's definitely real and you can make a lot of money from it – just ask Bill Gates.

A lot of corporate value these days is found in the likes of brand names or simply in the skills of the people who work for the group. These things can't be put on a balance sheet but they obviously have value.

The net asset value was quite a useful ratio in the old manu-facturing-based economy when most assets were tangible. In today's service-based and knowledge-based economy there are not many companies where the net asset approach is going to come in useful.

DIVIDEND YIELD

Shareholders have the right to receive dividends from a company and that gives us another approach to measuring share value. The dividend return on a share is rather like the interest income on a building society account, and can be worked out as a percentage. The calculation method is fairly simple. Take the net (after-tax) dividend and divide by the share price. Multiply the result by 100, and you have the dividend yield in percentage terms.

Take Acme Insurance, which pays a total dividend for the year of 6p per share and has a share price of 200p. Dividing 6 by 200 gives us 0.03. Multiplying the result by 100 gives us 3. The dividend yield on the shares is 3 per cent. So you might assume, as with a building society account, that the higher yield you get the better. But as George Gershwin wrote in *Porgy and Bess*, 'It ain't necessarily so'.

As with the price-earnings ratio, the market is always looking ahead to the future. Let us go back to our example of Go-Ahead and Stick-in-the-Mud. Go-Ahead has a price of 200p and a dividend of 6p so its yield is 3 per cent. Stick has a share price of 100p and a dividend of 5p so its yield is 5 per cent. Stick looks like the bargain.

But next year the market is forecasting that Go-Ahead will raise its dividend to 9p, taking its *prospective yield* to 4.5 per cent. Stick, in contrast, is expected to cut its dividend to 4p, reducing its prospective yield to 4 per cent. Now Go-Ahead looks like the bargain.

The general rule is that companies with a low dividend yield are those where dividends are expected to grow substantially over the long term. Investors are happy to accept a low return now in the hope of a higher return later on. These companies are usually in fast-growing industries such as mobile phones or software and they want to reinvest their money in the business rather than pay it out to shareholders.

Companies with high dividend yields usually fall into one of two categories. The first is slow-growing, mature businesses such as a water utility. Water profits are controlled by a regulator and so simply cannot grow too fast. But since we all need to use water, and will always do so, the companies can be pretty sure of their future profits. They can afford to pay out a large percentage of their current profits in the form of dividends and the shares can have a high yield.

The second group of high-yielders contains companies where the market is concerned about the company's future. Last year's dividend looks high in relation to the current share price but investors are concerned that next year's dividend will be cut or even eliminated altogether. If the share price yields more than 10 per cent, then the company normally falls into this category. The high yield thus indicates the high risk of holding these shares.

That said, a strategy of buying blue chips with above-average yields has proved quite successful in the past, in both the UK and the US. Sometimes markets can get too depressed about the prospects for a company and drive down the share price too far. As the price falls, the yield rises.

Take Acme Oil, which pays a dividend of 3p per share. At the start of the year the company's share price is 100p, so the shares yield 3 per cent. But the oil price falls sharply because of a warm winter in the Northern Hemisphere that cuts fuel consumption. Worried investors drive the Acme shares down to 50p. At that point, the shares yield 6 per cent.

The shares could now well be a bargain. Not only might the oil price rebound (next winter could be colder) but, provided the company can maintain its dividend, the shares provide a very decent income. In effect, investors are getting a 6 per cent yield (equivalent to a good savings account return) with the potential for capital gain on top.

The dividend yield has some advantages as a means of measuring share prices. Companies have to offer shareholders the right to receive dividends in cash, so the dividend is a good test of the 'real' profitability of a company. Profits can be fiddled but dividends cannot.

But there are also big problems with the yield valuation method. For a start, an increasing number of companies do not pay dividends at all. They prefer to reinvest all their profits in growing the business. Microsoft, for example, has never paid a dividend. Clearly, however, non-dividend-paying companies have a value, especially if they are making profits. A yield-based system would avoid such shares altogether.

A lot of investors will eventually want to take some sort of income from their share portfolios. But there are alternatives to dividends. One is simply to sell enough shares each year to use up the capital gains tax allowance. That will give investors a modest tax-free income. And since the tax rate on dividends is the same as the rate charged on capital gains, it does not really matter if the income-seeking investor sells more shares each year than the CGT allowance.

Companies also offer investors a way of taking income by indulging in share buy-back programmes. These involve the company using its own cash (or borrowing money) to buy back shares from investors. This allows investors who need income to do so by selling part of their holding. It also usually boosts the earnings per share of the company concerned. This is because companies can deduct the cost of interest payments from their tax bill whereas they cannot do the same with dividends.

Investors can find the price-earnings ratios and the dividend yields of quoted companies in the back pages of the second section of the *Financial Times* from Tuesday to Saturday.

CASH FLOW MEASURES

Another very useful approach to valuing shares is to look at the cash flow of the company. You may be surprised to learn that this can be quite different from a business's profits. Deciding a firm's level of profit is more an art than a science; for example, if you have a five-year contract, for which you are paid upfront, do you recognise all the profit in the first year? Or a fifth every year? Or all at the end? For this reason it can be easy for companies to manipulate profit figures. Cash flow is harder to manipulate. And it is, over the long run, more reliable. If profits are consistently higher than cash flow, investors should be suspicious.

So some investors ignore the price-earnings (P/E) ratio and use a price-to-cash flow ratio. Beginner investors will probably need help from a broker in calculating this. The lower the price-to-cash flow ratio, the better as far as a new investor is concerned. Price-to-cash flow ratio can also be very useful in comparing companies in different countries, since it avoids the difficulties of different accounting or tax treatments.

PRICE-TO-SALES

This is an alternative measure of valuation that can be used when companies, particularly those involved in the Internet, are not making any profits or paying any dividends.

The price-to-sales ratio relates the total market value of the group to total sales, or the sales per share to the share price.

Often Internet companies will be trading at a very high multiple of sales (sometimes hundreds, or even thousands of times) because investors expect sales to increase very rapidly in the future. It is far from an ideal measure (what good are sales if you don't make a profit on them?) but it at least allows for comparisons between companies in the same sector.

Price-to-sales ratios can also be used, on occasion, for bargain-hunting in the more traditional areas of the stock market. Sometimes the entire market value of a company can be worth much less than its sales. While this does not necessarily mean the shares are a bargain (often the company will be loss-making or earning a very small profit margin on each sale), it could mean that a change of management or approach might turn the company around. At least it is selling goods that somebody wants.

PRICE PER USER

This is another approach that is used to value Internet companies in particular. This measure relates the share price to the number of users of the site or service, and has often been used for Internet service providers (ISPs) such as Freeserve.

Again, the approach is far from ideal. Some users may provide little or no revenue; others a lot. But the central idea is that it allows comparisons between companies. While no one may know how much ISPs are really worth, it seems common sense to suggest an ISP with 2 million users is worth more than one with 1 million.

PEG RATIO

This measure divides the price-earnings ratio by the growth rate of corporate profits/earnings per share. Ideally the growth rate should cover several years, including the rate forecast by brokers for the next year or two. The PEG ratio is a refinement of the price-earnings ratio explained earlier in the chapter. It is designed to help investors find growth companies that look undervalued.

The lower the ratio the better. Ideally, investors would like a company whose earnings are growing at 50 per cent a year and which trades on a P/E of just 10. That would represent a PEG of 0.2. There is no universally agreed ideal PEG, but investors tend to prefer the ratio to be below 1 and a PEG of 0.5 or so may indicate that the shares are a bargain. Once the PEG starts to get above 2, then the shares are starting to look expensive: do you really want to pay a P/E of 50 for a company growing at only 20 per cent a year?

Again this ratio allows investors to compare one company with another. If two companies are both growing at 15 per cent a year, then the one on a P/E of 20 should, other things being equal, be more of a bargain than the one on a P/E of 30.

Unlike price-earnings ratios and dividend yields, getting information on ratios such as PEGs and price per sales is more difficult. There are specialist services, such as *Company Refs* (published by Hemmington Scott), which provide the data – at a price. An advisory stockbroker should also be able to get the information for you.

It is worth remembering one thing in this blizzard of ratios and statistics. A share is worth what someone else will pay for it. That will vary with the mood of the market. Over the years, the average P/E and dividend yield has fluctuated quite sharply through recessions, wars and periods of high infla- tion. Shares have tended to be rated very highly in recent years because of more stable economic growth, low inflation and hopes that new technology will transform corporate profits.

TIMING THE MARKET
Aside from picking a particular share, how do you decide

when is a good time to put money into the stock market? Share prices can be very volatile at times and it would be much better to invest just after, rather than just before, a 20 per cent drop.

As I have emphasised throughout this book, investing in shares is the best way of making money over the long term. So provided you can leave your money in the stock market for at least five years or so, you probably do not need to worry about timing your investment. But some people want to put their money into equities for less than five years. And most would like to feel they could get their money out quickly if they needed it.

There are plenty of people who pontificate on the level of the market for a living. The first thing to say is that most of them must be wrong, most of the time. If it was obvious that the stock market was overvalued, then investors would already have sold their shares, and prices would have fallen until the market did not look overvalued.

That said, market tops sometimes do look obvious in retrospect, normally by reference to the same measures investors use to evaluate individual shares. At the peak of the market in 1987, for example, the US stock market was trading at one of its highest ever (until then) price-earnings ratios and its lowest ever dividend yields.

One can work out a price-earnings ratio for the overall market just as one can for individual shares. (To save time, you can find the figures on the back page of the second section of the *Financial Times* every Tuesday to Friday.)

As a general rule, you would have done very well to have bought into the stock market when it was trading on a historic price-earnings ratio of less than 10, and to have sold when it was more than 20. But that rule would not have worked in the late 1990s. The P/E on the All-Share passed 20 in early

1998 and, although there was a nasty dip in the late summer of that year, investors still gained 34 per cent over the next two years.

The same problem has occurred with the idea of using the dividend yield as an overall market indicator. The yield on the All-Share dipped below 3 per cent in early 1998, a level it had only previously reached just before the crash of 1987. With the benefit of hindsight, that was a worrying sign. Over the next three years, the market effectively went nowhere. But in the short term, the yield was not a useful signal. The market reached an all-time high at the end of 1999 before falling back.

The problem with both those measures is that they are nominal figures; in other words, they take no account of the level of inflation. During the 1970s and 1980s inflation was very high by historical standards, and it made sense for investors to demand a much higher dividend yield in nominal terms. With inflation much lower in the 1990s, investors were willing to accept a much lower nominal dividend yield. (They have also been getting income from other sources, such as share buy-backs and takeovers.) A 2.5 per cent dividend yield at a time of 2.5 per cent inflation is worth just the same, in real terms, as a 5 per cent yield in a world of 5 per cent inflation.

Lower inflation also encourages investors to accept a higher price-earnings ratio. If you turn the P/E on its head, you get a ratio called the *earnings yield* (earnings per share divided by the share price). Expressed as a percentage, one can view this as the 'return' from equities. Again, investors should be willing to accept a lower nominal earnings yield (and higher P/E) if inflation is low, provided that the real return is still positive.

An alternative approach is to compare equities with other

assets, such as bond yields or the return from cash deposits. The advantage of this approach is that nominal bond yields and short-term interest rates tend to fall and rise in line with inflation.

One ratio compares the bond yield on long-term gilts with the dividend yield. (You can also find this ratio on the London Stock Markets page of the *FT*.)

This approach is based on the fact that investors have a choice between owning shares, bonds or cash. If they opt for shares, they get a low level of income but they hope for capital gains. However, if the income from bonds or cash is high enough, they will be tempted to switch. Furthermore, higher bond yields and short-term interest rates normally mean a slower economy – and that is bad news for corporate profits.

So a high bond yield, relative to the dividend yield, means shares are expensive; a low ratio means they are cheap. The rule of thumb is supposedly that, if the ratio dips below 2, then investors should opt for equities.

A similar calculation compares the bond yield with the earnings yield. This gets round the objection that dividends are less important for investors these days. Again, the higher the bond yield relative to the earnings yield, the greater the incentive for investors to sell shares and buy bonds. If the ratio is low, then the growth attractions of shares are likely to have more appeal.

In the UK this ratio peaked at around 2 in the summer of 1987, which did indeed turn out to be a bad time to buy shares. It dropped below 1 in October 1998, which was a good time to invest in equities.

Many analysts would argue, however, that the above comparisons are based on a false premise. One should not compare equities, a real asset whose returns are protected from inflation (because the value of corporate assets and profits should go up in line with prices over the long run), with bonds, a nominal asset whose value is eaten away by inflation. A much better comparison for equities is index-linked bonds, they argue. These bonds are issued by several governments, including the US and the UK. Both the repayment value and annual interest payments are guaranteed to keep pace with inflation.

The rule of thumb is that if the dividend yield is higher on the market than the yield on index-linked then shares are good value and vice versa. At the time of writing, the yield on UK index-linked gilts was just over 2 per cent, which gave some support to share prices.

However, this measure may also be less than perfect. The UK government's budget surplus means that it has issued very few index-linked gilts in recent years. Meanwhile there are lots of pension funds that see the bonds as a useful safe-guard against inflation. This has driven up prices (and down yields) in the sector and may have distorted the comparison with equities.

All this goes to prove my initial point, that there is no sure way of timing the market. Aside from these quantitative measures, however, there are also some qualitative factors that may help you decide when to buy shares.

At the bottom of a bear market:

Everybody is bearish Investors are no longer interested in buying shares, preferring safer options such as bonds and cash. There is little coverage of the stock market in mainstream media. There is lots of gloom about the economy.

Valuations are low The price-earnings ratio will be below and the dividend yield above the long-term average. But many analysts will argue that they could go lower still.

Money's too tight to mention Interest rates will be high, banks will be unwilling to lend money or consumers will be unwilling to take on debt. It could be any combination of the above factors but the key will be that very little borrowing will be occurring; everyone will be risk-averse.

Bargains will abound There will be lots of stocks available at severely depressed prices but investors will generally be too cautious to take advantage. Good quality companies may trade at less than asset value or on double-digit percentage yields.

The top of a bull market tends to be characterised by the following:

Everyone is highly optimistic Shares are seen as the ideal investment, with little or no risk. Forecasts are for the FTSE 100 to gain 20 per cent or more over the year. There is plenty of coverage of the stock market in the mainstream media. People you meet talk about their investment plans and share tips; someone you know has made a lot of money from equities.

Valuations are very high The price-earnings ratio is well above, and the dividend yield well below, the historical average. But analysts say such valuations are justified. There is talk of a 'new era'.

Money is plentiful It is easy to borrow money and people are doing so to expand their businesses, finance their consumer purchases, buy bigger houses or even invest in shares. Interest rates are low, although they may be rising.

Bargains are difficult to find There are very few stocks trading at below asset value or at ratios traditional investors would consider as cheap. Some stocks trade at very high valuations but people buy them in any case in hopes of making quick speculative gains.

In short, when the outlook is incredibly rosy and everyone is involved in the market, then beware: there may be nobody left to buy. And when the outlook is unremittingly gloomy and hardly anyone is involved in the market, then take advantage of it: there may be nobody with stock left to sell, as everyone who wanted to sell has already done so.

CONSTANT RATIO PLAN

One approach to investment strategy that is designed to help with market timing is a *constant ratio plan*, based on set allocations of your total funds.

The first step is to devise some sort of ideal ratio for your portfolio, say 60 per cent shares and 40 per cent bonds. This ratio will vary according to your circumstances: your need for income, your aversion to risk, and so on.

One rule of thumb is that the proportion of bonds in your portfolio should be the same as your age, so that it gradually increases over time as you approach retirement.

Say you start with savings of £10,000, made up of £6,000 of shares and £4,000 of bonds. The next step is to adjust your holdings in response to market movements. Say that your shares rise in value by 20 per cent and your bonds fall by 5 per cent. You would now have £11,000 in total, split £7,200 in shares and £3,800 in bonds. Your portfolio would now have a 65 per cent weighting in shares and only 35 per cent in bonds. That would break the ideal ratio. So the answer is to sell £600 worth of shares and invest the proceeds in bonds. This would take you to £6,600/£4,400 or a 60/40 split.

The principle behind this approach is that you are always buying things that have fallen in price and selling things that have risen. This gives you an automatic way of taking profits and ensures you do not get over-exposed to an overvalued market. The snag is that, since shares tend to perform better than bonds over the long term, this portfolio will not give you as high returns as a fund that invests 100 per cent in equities.

But the portfolio will be less risky. You should be protected against sharp falls in the value of your holdings; if the stock market crashes, bond prices rise as investors seek out a 'safe haven' investment.

Another problem with this strategy is the danger of 'over-trading'. You could end up forever fiddling with your portfolio as the share proportion shifts, say, from 59 to 61 per cent and back again. The result would be a high level of dealing costs that would reduce your investment performance. The best way of getting round this problem is to trade only on the basis of some set rules. Either:

(1) only adjust the portfolio if the proportions get substantially out of line, say at least 5 per cent from the target; or

(2) only adjust the portfolio at set intervals, say every quarter or every year.

I deliberately chose a simple portfolio split to help explain the concept, but the same idea can be used with more variables. An investor could have set proportions of equities, bonds and cash, or split the equity portion into UK and overseas, or even by sectors. The key is the discipline the method brings to the portfolio, with the aim of buying low and selling high.

CHAPTER SEVEN

TECHNICAL ANALYSIS: USING CHARTS TO PREDICT FUTURE PRICE MOVEMENT

TECHNICAL analysts believe that it's possible to predict the future movement of a share's price by observing its historical patterns. While this may sound a bit like reading goat entrails or tea leaves, and has proven just as controversial, more and more people are using technical analysis as a predictive tool to 'time' the market in the short term. (In contrast, fundamental analysis is used primarily to predict share prices over the long term.)

There are many different types of technical analysts, who are also known as chartists. Some of them look for specific trends that have produced predictable reactions, such as a 'head and shoulders' or 'double top' curve on a performance graph (which I'll explain below). Others believe that price movements follow consistent patterns: for example, five up waves and three down waves on a graph. Others, instead of focusing on a single day's price movement, prefer to look at charts that 'smooth out' the daily volatility by charting each day the average movement of the most recent past twenty, thirty or ninety days and trying to spot when a trend will change.

Behind each of these techniques is the belief that what really governs price movements is not rational calculation but investor emotion. It is not uncommon, for example, for investors to leap on to passing bandwagons. A horde of investors will suddenly buy shares that have started to go up in price. But the moment the trend threatens to change, they are just as quick to jump off the bandwagon and dump the shares. If you could accurately predict this behaviour, as the technical analysts believe they can, then you'd be well positioned to make a lot of money.

But technical analysis has caused sharp divisions within the investment community. There are plenty of people who believe the technique is mumbo-jumbo, that chartists only tell you 'shares are going up when they are going up, and that they are coming down when they are coming down.' And they have a point. Too often, chartists will offer incomprehensible bits of advice like: 'If the market falls below 5,011, we could be headed into a bear phase, unless resistance holds at 5,006, in which case we expect a near-term target of 5,122.' Now, does this mean you should be ready to sell or buy? Your interpretation is probably as valid as mine! There is an old saying in the investment community that you should keep in mind: if you give ten analysts the same information, you won't get a consensus, you'll get an argument. In short, all interpretations are relative.

Investors should also be cautious about 'sure-fire' trading systems that promise you riches on the condition that you follow certain trading recommendations provided by a computer programme. If the system is so 'sure-fire', then how come the sellers are passing it on to you rather than using it themselves to make millions? The only sure thing about such advice is that you will most likely lose a lot of money trading, and the company that devised the system will make a lot of money selling it.

That said, there are many serious private and institutional investors who use charts to make money. And in some markets, such as foreign exchange and commodity futures, traders spend a lot of time paying attention to them.

One of the reasons that technical analysis has grown in popularity is that research techniques based on fundamentals, such as looking at earnings per share, P/E ratio or cash flow, have been unsuccessful in predicting share price movements in the short term. It obviously makes sense that, over the long term, a company's earnings and assets must be linked to the performance of the share price. But in the short term the technical analysts may have a point, and factors such as investor psychology may be more important.

Consider, for example, the big run-up in UK technology shares in the last three months of 1999 and the first two months of 2000. Was that really prompted by a change in the fundamentals of the technology sector? And if so, did the fundamentals then deteriorate sharply in the spring of 2000? I doubt it. It seems more likely that the fundamentals stayed pretty much the same, but what changed sharply was investors' perceptions about those shares. Those changing perceptions are something the chartists hope to capture in their graphs, and take advantage of in their own trades.

The four most commonly used types of chart are the line, bar, point and figure, and moving average charts.

LINE CHART

The most basic type of graph is the line chart, a familiar illustration that you will see in daily papers everywhere. Most line charts use closing daily prices, but you can also look at the movement of an index or share price at various time intervals – e.g. minute by minute, hour by hour. Line charts may have nothing to do with finance; they may simply show the opinion poll rating of the government over the last two years. But a typical chart in the *Financial Times* would show the progress of the FTSE 100 index over the past year. This will give you a good impression of how the market has been behaving, graphically demonstrating whether it has gone straight up, plunged after an initial rise, or bounced around in a narrow range.

Figure 7.1 Line Chart

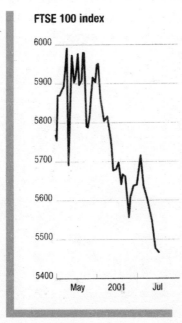

Financial Times, July 2001

BAR CHART

A bar chart provides more detailed information about a stock's or the market's daily movement. Rather than simply recording the daily closing price, this chart captures three elements of price movement: the high and low for the day (joined together by a vertical line) and the closing price (indicated by a horizontal dash at the appropriate point on the line). A bar chart thus looks like a series of elongated 't's. The length of the vertical line gives you a visual image of the price swing during a session as investors react to news about a specific company or the overall market.

Figure 7.2 Bar Chart

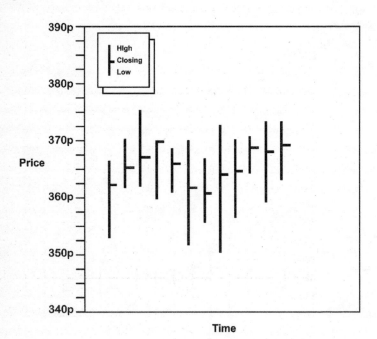

POINT-AND-FIGURE CHART

A point-and-figure chart shows the daily volatility of share prices in some detail. The price movement is recorded on a grid of boxes. Each box in a column represents a distinct price movement (1p, etc.) with Xs showing the upward price movement and Os showing the downward price movement. So, using a grid as shown in Figure 7.3 in which each vertical box represents 10p, if Acme Insurance rose from 330p to 390p at the start of trading, this price movement would be represented by six Xs moving upward in the first column. If the price then fell to 340p, you would move over to the next vertical column and the chart would show four Os descending in the first column, and so on. The graph therefore only records the up and down movements. It does not record

Figure 7.3 Point-and-Figure Chart

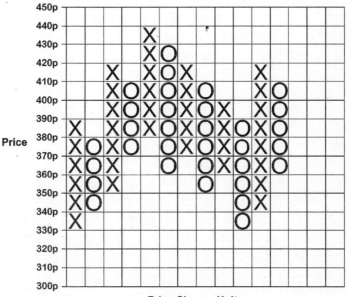

Price

Price Change Units

(1) the time taken to make the price move or (2) the volume of trading. Analysts who use point-and-figure charts are interested only in recording the fact that price changes occur. The degree or percentage of the price change (as an indicator of continued movement in the same direction or a change of direction) is more important than when it occurs.

MOVING AVERAGE CHART

Moving average charts (also known as rolling averages) are used to smooth out a stock's or the market's daily movement and to enable analysts to focus on the market's overall trend. The moving average is computed using a stock's or the market's average closing prices over a fixed period of time (e.g., twenty days, thirty days, ninety days). The average is recomputed each day to include the current day's closing price within the fixed period. This number is then charted on a graph.

Where do you find such charts? If you can get access to the data, you can compile them yourself. Or you can buy them from a charting service, and some brokers may pass on their charting research. The Internet has greatly improved private investor access to chart data, and you can find charts at sites such as *www.alphachart.com* and *www.askresearch.com*. There are also software packages that you can buy so you can construct your own charts.

INTERPRETING CHARTS

One of the most basic approaches is to look for emerging trends. An old piece of market folklore is that 'the trend is your friend'. If shares are in an uptrend (when successive peaks and troughs tend to be higher than the one before), that is said to be a good time to buy shares. But if the trend is down, that is a bad time to buy and a good time to sell.

An alternative is a trading range in which a share price moves between two set points. A trading range will often have a *resistance level*, a high point above which the price seems unable to go, and a *support level*, a point below which the price seems unwilling to fall. Once those points have been established they can become self-fulfilling prophecies, as technical analysts sell as the price approaches the resistance point and buy when the price begins to reach the support level.

Figure 7.5 Resistance and Support Levels of a Trading Range

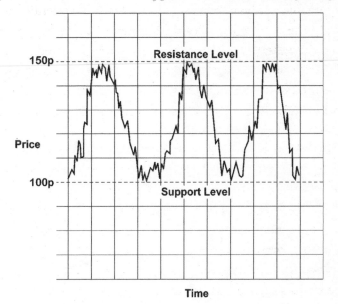

Technical analysts have two theories about resistance and support levels. First, if the price manages to pass above (what the chartists call a breakout) a resistance level, then the price will continue to go upwards. A break above a resistance level is therefore seen as bullish. And second, if the market falls below a support, then the price will continue to go down. Falling below a support level is seen as bearish.

The old resistance and support levels may switch roles once a breakout occurs. Suppose that Acme Insurance has been trading between 100p and 150p as shown in Figure 7.5, with the former seen as a support level and the later as a resistance level. If the price rises to 160p, then that old resistance level of 150p may become the support level for a new trading range, say 150–200p. And if the price falls to 90p, then the old support level of 100p may become a resistance level for a range of 50–100p.

Figure 7.6 Head-and-Shoulders Formation

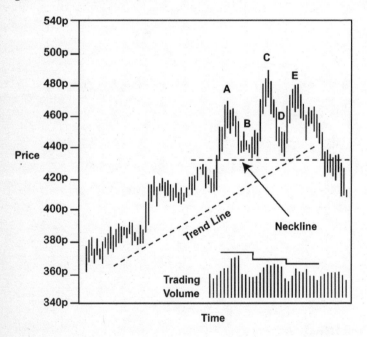

Among the patterns that technical analysts look for when charting a stock or an index is a head-and-shoulders formation. Nothing to do with dandruff shampoo, this pattern is considered a reversal pattern and consists of three peaks (see Figure 7.6). The first and third peaks (A and E in the graph) are lower than the middle peak C, thus forming the head (C) and shoulders (A and E) outline. In between those peaks, the price dips to the troughs B and D, which should be roughly at the same level, and form the 'neckline' of the pattern. Chartists believe that a head-and-shoulders pattern represents the reversal of an uptrend as the market runs out of steam. This loss of momentum is indicated by a drop in trading volume during the second rally that forms the head of the pattern. The decline in volume continues during the formation of the second shoulder. The share price is expected to fall by as much as the distance between the head and the neckline. A head and shoulders pattern is a bearish indicator.

Figure 7.7 Inverted Head-and-Shoulders Formation

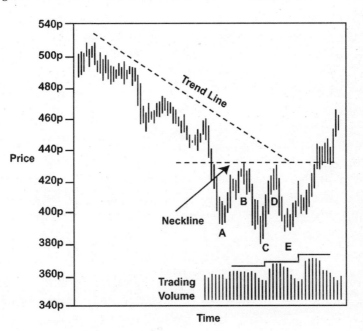

In contrast, an inverted head-and-shoulders (Figure 7.7) consists of three successive troughs of which the second is the deepest. This formation is a bullish indicator, signalling the reversal of a downtrend. In this pattern, the trading volume increases during the formation of the head and continues to increase during the formation of the second shoulder.

Other patterns that also indicate a reversal of a trend are a double top (Figure 7.8) and a double bottom (Figure 7.9). In the first case, two successive tops are recorded showing a pattern on the chart rather like an 'm'. The market's failure

Figure 7.8 Double Top Formation

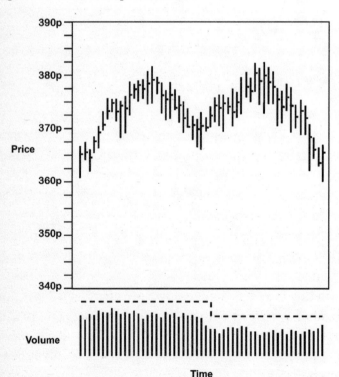

Figure 7.9 Double Bottom Formation

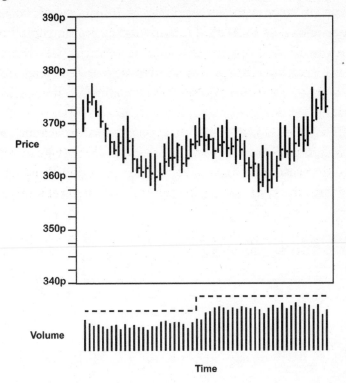

to break through a price barrier (similar to a resistance level) combined with lower trading volume confirms that a double top is bearish. It indicates a reversal of an uptrend. A double bottom signals the reversal of a downtrend. As the second bottom is formed there is a simultaneous increase in the trading volume. The market should therefore continue to move higher.

Interpreting moving averages involves comparing the price movement of a share to both a short-term average (10- or 20-day) and a long-term one (90- or 200-day). If a share price suddenly breaks above a long-term average and this movement is confirmed by a short-term average also breaking above that average, then it is interpreted as a bullish indicator for the stock. The short-term average will be above the long-term average if the highest prices have occurred in the most recent days. A bearish indicator would be indicated if the short-term average drops below the long-term average at the same time that the share price drops below the average. In both the bullish and bearish scenarios, if the share price does not follow the moving averages then there is a potential for a false breakout.

But there are many schools of technical analysis, each of which tends to believe it is following the 'true faith' and to regard the others as non-believers. Elliott wave theorists, for example, believe the markets follow a set pattern of up and down waves. In the bull phase, there are five waves, of which the first, third and fifth see prices rising while the second and fourth see them falling. In the bearish phase, there are three waves, of which the first and third see falling prices and the second sees rising prices. Understandably, this can lead to some confusion, and even dispute, when analysts are trying to decide whether a setback in prices is, say, one of the two down waves of the uptrend or of the downtrend.

Whether you believe any of this technical analysis will be a matter of personal taste. And before attempting to use any of these approaches, you should devote a lengthy period of study to the matter by reading a specialist book on the subject, so that you can recognise the chart patterns, understand their implications, and do the maths with ease.

It would be sensible to begin your career as a chartist by trading a notional portfolio to test and learn how the system works on paper before using your own, very real money. And remember to allow for costs: every time you trade you will face broker's commission, the bid-offer spread, stamp duty and so on. The more you trade, the higher your costs will be.

CHAPTER EIGHT

INVESTMENT STRATEGIES

How do I get started? What is the best strategy for making money from investing? As a beginning investor, don't fall into the trap of trying to create your own unique investment strategy or methodology. Stay with investment strategies that are tried and true. The first three strategies outlined below are those that all of us should consider. Others listed under speculative strategies are here for explanatory purposes only. Since so many people ask about them I felt they had to be discussed in this chapter. However, I do not believe that these speculative strategies are suitable for beginning investors. Hopefully understanding them will help you *not* yield to temptation until you are a much more experienced investor.

TRIED AND TRUE STRATEGIES

BUY AND HOLD

This is the classic strategy used by most long-term investors, and one most associated with famed investor Warren Buffett. This is not a sexy strategy. It is highly unlikely that you will be able to go to your local pub and buy everyone a pint with your one-day gains. Instead this strategy is about building wealth slowly and conservatively. Don't mistake these two words to mean that there is no risk. You can still choose companies whose share prices decline. But at least you are less likely to get caught up in the latest investment fad.

You use fundamental analysis to implement this strategy. You look for companies whose long-term growth prospects are solid. Such companies would have had steady increases in earnings and/or dividends over a long period of time, have products whose identity and market are global, a strong focus on new product development, and a business you can understand. The emphasis is on long-term consistency, instead of what's hot now. Once you've identified the companies, you buy them and keep them for as long as their prospects remain positive.

The buy-and-hold strategy should not be confused with what I call the sleeping beauty strategy – i.e., buying stocks, putting them away for years, and then suddenly finding the long-ignored shares, which are now worth a gazillion pounds. You must employ minimal vigilance throughout the time you are holding the stock. You don't have to read the financial news every day, but periodically (quarterly, semi-annually or annually) you should review the company's performance, financial stability, earnings growth, dividends and prospects for the future. If there are signs that the company is entering a bad phase, don't be afraid to sell. You don't have to reinvest this money immediately. Instead you can keep it liquid and patiently wait for the next investment opportunity.

During the time you are holding shares, you should take advantages of the features discussed below that some companies offer investors. These can help increase your return.

Scrip dividends Rather than receive those small dividend cheques from the company in which you have invested, find out if the company offers scrip dividends. These permit investors to reinvest their dividends automatically in additional shares of the company. To find out if a company in which you have invested offers this service, contact their shareholder services division and find out the details.

The primary advantage of scrip dividends is compounding: you begin earning dividends on the dividends that you have reinvested in the company. And over the long term this essentially passive investment strategy can yield a nice gain, especially if the general trend in the stock's price movement is upward.

Scrip or bonus issues Keep in mind that not all companies pay dividends or offer scrip dividends. Even without these, the number of shares that a long-term, buy-and-hold investor owns can increase through periodic scrip issues. As the price of stock becomes 'too expensive' (this is a subjective evaluation), the company's board of directors may vote to offer a scrip (or bonus) issue (e.g., 2 for 1, 4 for 5, 3 for 1). The objective of a scrip issue is to make the securities more attractive to a wider range of investors. After a scrip issue or stock split, you own more shares in the company but the overall value of your holding will be unaffected since the share price will fall to reflect the greater number of shares in issue. While the share price drops when the scrip issue occurs, you have a greater number of shares on which to make money if the share's price continues to rise.

There is no pre-determined price at which all scrip issues occur. And there is no iron-clad rule about whether it is best to buy a stock before or after a scrip issue. Remember that with the buy-and-hold objective, your focus is on the long-term growth of the company.

Recouping your initial investment A common practice among many buy-and-hold investors is to recoup their initial investment at some point. Usually after the price of the stock has increased substantially or after the shares have split and then increased in value, some investors sell enough shares to get back the money they used to make the initial purchase. Other investors sell enough shares to recoup their initial investment plus any interest the money would have earned in a savings account. The sales proceeds are typically returned to the investor's savings account where they earn interest with no risk. The logic and advantage of this practice are clear and simple. The initial money invested has been returned (with or without interest) to a safe, risk-free bank account. The remaining stock position is supported totally by the profits made on the original investment. If the stock's price declines or the company goes bankrupt, then the investor has lost only the profits. Having recouped the initial investment and placed that money in a bank, the investor is realistically in the same position he or she would have been in if the original money had simply been deposited in a bank or building society.

POUND-COST AVERAGING

Pound-cost averaging is a long-term strategy whereby you invest the same amount of money in a unit trust at regular intervals – every two weeks, monthly or quarterly. You buy the security without considering its market price at the time of each purchase. Consistency in the amount being invested and the regularity of the payments is essential to the success of pound-cost averaging in order to minimise pricing and time risk.

Pound-cost averaging works on a simple principle. When the price of the unit trust declines, the fixed amount of money being invested buys more units. Hence, the purchasing power of your money expands. When the price of the unit trust rises, the fixed amount buys fewer units. Consequently, your money's purchasing power contracts. Over the long term, you will discover that the cost of each unit is lower than the average price per share during the investment period. Yes, I know this sounds totally confusing. And if you are at all phobic about maths, your mind just lapsed into reject mode, fear mode or coma mode. But before you go too far in one of these mindsets, take a deep breath, and look at the simple example in Figure 8.1. It shows how pound-cost averaging would work if you invested £250 each month over a one-year period – a total of £3,000 per year. When you invest your money each month, the value of the unit trust varies due to normal market price fluctuation. Pay careful attention to the difference between the average *cost* per unit and the average *price* per unit in the explanation that follows.

Over the twelve-month period, you invest a total of £3,000 (£250 × 12) and purchase a total of 241.96 units. The average cost of buying these units is computed using the following formula: *total amount invested ÷ total number of units bought*. The average cost per unit is £12.39 (£3,000 ÷ 241.96).

The average price per unit, shown in the third column is computed using a different formula: *total unit prices for the period ÷ number of investments*. The average price per unit is £12.92 (£155 ÷ 12). Each unit, therefore, cost 53 pence (£12.92 – £12.39) less than the average price for the twelve-month period. Given the fact that all unit trusts fluctuate in value daily, pound-cost averaging virtually guarantees that your cost basis will always be lower than the average price per unit.

The fact that the average cost is lower than the average price does not mean that you have a guaranteed gain. (Note: if you misinterpreted the final sentence in the previous paragraph to mean that pound-cost averaging guarantees a

Figure 8.1 Illustrating the potential benefits of pound-cost averaging

MONTH	POUNDS INVESTED	PRICE PER UNIT	NO. OF UNITS BOUGHT
1	250	12.50	20.00
2	250	11.00	22.72
3	250	10.00	25.00
4	250	13.00	19.23
5	250	9.50	26.32
6	250	9.00	27.28
7	250	12.00	20.83
8	250	14.00	17.86
9	250	15.50	16.13
10	250	17.50	14.29
11	250	15.00	16.67
12	250	16.00	15.63
TOTAL NUMBER OF PAYMENTS	TOTAL £ INVESTED	AVERAGE PRICE PER UNIT	TOTAL UNITS BOUGHT
12	£3,000	£12.92 (£155 ÷ 12)	241.96

gain, it may be a significant indicator that you are looking for a magic investment formula. Such a sure-fire formula does not exist.) If a unit trust's price trends downwards during the implementation of pound-cost averaging, the average cost will still be lower than the average price; however, if you were to sell the units at the lower market price you have a loss on your investment, not a gain. Look at the first six months investment in the table above and you will see an example of this fact. The price of the security drops from £12.50 to £9.00. The average price per unit during this period is £10.83 (£65÷6). The average cost per unit is £10.67 (£1,500÷140.55), 16 pence lower than the average price.

Pound-cost averaging works in both a declining market and a rising market, and its benefits can be enhanced when combined with a scrip dividend. However, the strategy offers no guarantees that you will make a profit on the investment or be protected against a loss.

There are several disadvantages to this method of investing. First, pound-cost averaging can limit your profits during a rising market in comparison to investing a large sum at once. If the price of a unit trust increases sharply with only small reversals or declines, then the average cost per unit will most likely be higher than the market price of the unit when the strategy was started. In this case, pound-cost averaging limits your gain. You would have had a greater profit by investing all the money at once.

This disadvantage is of minimal concern to most investors, however, for two reasons. First, pound-cost averaging is the primary way that people with modest capital can begin investing regularly in the stock market. Typically, this person is able to invest only a small sum at a time. The long-term objective is to build up a substantial amount of money. And, second, the relationship between the initial cost and the average cost varies according to the market price fluctuations during the investment period. For each investor, the specific benefits of pound-cost averaging will be somewhat different, depending on the length of time, and the amount of money invested.

Like the buy-and-hold strategy, pound-cost averaging starts from the basic premise that the price or value of unit trusts tend to increase over the long term. The success of this strategy depends on your discipline in adhering to the following principles:

(1) Invest over a long period of time. With a long time horizon (seven to ten years is typical), you will experience the occasional downturns in the market that will enable the buying power of your money to expand, thereby increasing the benefits of this strategy.

(2) Invest at regular intervals: every two weeks, monthly, or quarterly.

(3) Invest regardless of the price of the unit trust.

(4) Choose high-quality unit trusts, those with good long-term performance histories.

In addition you should have sufficient fortitude to stick to the plan through the highs and lows of the market.

CORE AND EXPLORE

This strategy is appropriate if you are a conservative, growth-oriented investor whose primary objective is preservation of capital. It is also a good strategy for anyone just beginning to learn about and invest in the stock market.

The logic underlying core and explore is as uncomplicated as its rhyme. First, this strategy assumes that you, as an investor, are willing to tolerate volatility and risk that is *no greater than* that of the overall stock market as measured by indices such as the FTSE 100 share index or the FTSE All Share index. And second, it assumes that you also want to invest in specific business sectors or individual companies that have above-average growth prospects, but involve more risk than you are willing to take with the majority of your investment money. To implement this strategy, you divide your portfolio into two parts: the 'core' part and the 'explore' part.

The 'core' of your portfolio holds the majority of your money and serves as the moderately conservative foundation. This money *must* be invested in a vehicle that is well diversified and low risk. The easiest and most cost-efficient way to meet these requirements is to put the money in a unit trust or an OEIC (open-ended investment company). Either of the two types of unit trusts or OEICS listed below are generally recommended.

(1) *An established, well-diversified, large-capitalisation, managed unit trust or OEIC with a good long-term track record* While most of your choices in this group will be domestic equity funds, you can also use other funds with the same features. Importantly, the volatility of the fund you select should not be significantly more than that of the overall stock market as measured by a benchmark index; or,

(2) *A tracker fund or OEIC that follows a broad market measure* Tracker funds are available today that track the performance and total return of most major indices. Overall, funds in this group are attractive because of their low expenses.

By placing the majority of your money in one of these types of funds, you get several benefits. First, it brakes your (and every investor's) natural tendency to concentrate too much money in one sector, especially if that sector is in the news and producing impressive gains. Thus buying one of the funds listed above prevents you from getting caught up in a trend – as many people did in 1999 and 2000 when technology and internet shares were hot – that could result in significant losses. Second, you subject your money – as well as your nerves – to less severe ups and downs. After all, a well-diversified, large-capitalisation unit trust or OEIC is usually much less volatile that the majority of individual shares. Therefore, as stabilisers are to ocean liners during rough seas, so will the core fund be to the value of your port-folio during turbulent markets. Moments of high anxiety about your investments may, hopefully, be fewer – or at least smoother.

The 'explore' portion of your portfolio is the money that remains after you have chosen the unit trust or OEIC that will be your portfolio's core. It's up to you to determine the percentage of your investable assets that should be used 'to explore'. A key consideration is your risk tolerance: how would you feel if you lost this part of your investment? You invest this money in the stock of specific companies or in those business sectors (using sector funds) that your research shows are most likely to produce gains better than those of the overall stock market. In short, you get to test your skill as a stock or sector picker, using a smaller percentage of your total assets.

If your selections do well, they will boost the return of your total portfolio. Indeed, the yield from your core fund combined with higher gains from your sector fund or indi-vidual shares can result in your portfolio having a total return that is better than that from the overall stock market. This is the holy grail of the core-and-explore strategy: an overall higher return without a significant increase in risk. On the other hand, if your 'exploring' results in significant losses, it should have two effects – one certain, the other probable. First, the losses will certainly reduce the combined total return from the two parts of your portfolio. And second (this is the probable part), you may realise that you lack the skills, discipline, insights and nerves required to choose and analyse individual stock or sector funds. If your losses have been insignificant, then count your blessings: you've gained this insight about your skills – or lack thereof – quickly and cheaply, without exposing the majority of your assets to this additional risk.

The core-and-explore strategy is easy to understand and easy to implement. Beginning investors, in particular, can use it regardless of the amount of money they have to invest. As a novice, your starting point is the unit trust or OEIC that will be your portfolio's core. Begin by putting all your money into that fund. After you reach your predetermined threshold, you can begin putting a percentage of your money in a sector fund or accumulating cash in an interest-paying account that you will use to buy individual stocks. While core and explore is an easy strategy, it is not a mindless strategy. You must monitor the performance of your investments to make sure that they are providing the return that you wish, given your risk tolerance.

SPECULATIVE STRATEGIES

SPREAD BETTING

A spread bet is a relatively new and increasingly popular way to invest in the stock market, and it will be familiar to those who gamble on sport. In this wager, you bet on whether a number will be above or below 'the spread', a given range of numbers.

Say, for example, you want to bet on the number of goals scored by Alan Shearer in a season. The spread might be 14–17. If you believe he will score more than 17 goals, you will place an up bet. If you believe he will score fewer than 14, you will place a down bet. The big difference from a conventional bet, however, is that these are not fixed odds. Let's say you bet £5 per goal. If you have been an optimist, you will make £5 for every goal Alan Shearer scores above 17, *but you will lose £5 for every goal he falls short*. Your maximum loss is thus £85 (17 times £5). Your maximum gain? Well, if Shearer equalled Dixie Dean's all-time record of 60 goals in a season, you might make £215 (43 times £5).

Note that if Alan Shearer's goal tally falls within the spread (from 14 to 17), then both those who bet high and those who bet low will lose money. If he scores 15, then those who bet high at £5 a goal will lose £10, and those who bet low will lose £5. In other words, you can make a lot of money in spread betting, but you can lose a lot. This is not the same as putting £5 on an outsider in the Derby.

In financial spread betting, you are wagering on certain market indices – the FTSE 100, the Dow Jones Industrial Average, the NASDAQ Composite and so on – or on leading share prices. Let's say you bet on the FTSE 100. The bets cover three-month periods, so you might be betting on the index's level in, say, June. The spread will be above the current level of the index. (This reflects the fact that the betting company has to cover your bet in the financial futures market. Futures prices are higher than cash prices because of the time value of money.) Say the cash level is 6,000 and the spread is 6,060–6,090. You can thus bet that the market will be higher than 6,090 or lower than 6,060 by the time the bet ends. Say you placed an up bet of £5 per point. If, by the end of the period, the index reached 7,090, then you would have won £5,000. But if it fell to 5,090, you would have lost the same sum.

This is a serious, risky business. There are normally minimum betting levels of at least 50p a point. Given that an index can easily move 1,000 points in a few weeks, you should not be prepared to make a financial spread bet unless you can afford to lose several hundred pounds. Remember also that spread bets are enforceable in law, unlike other gambling debts.

There are some ways, however, of limiting your loss. Some spread betting companies will allow you to put in a 'stop loss' so that if the index moves, say, 200 points against you, your bet will automatically be closed out. (The snag with this strategy is that you get no chance to recoup your losses. Say you correctly assess that the market is due for a bull run but the market dips 200 points before rising 1,000. Your bet will be closed before your judgement is proved right.)

It is also worth noting that you do not have to sit passively until the closing date for the bet. At any time you can take your profits or cut your losses by placing the same bet in the opposite direction.

Say, in the above example, that the market had moved up 200 points so that the spread was 6,260–6,290. You now place a down bet of £5 per point. Whatever level the index reaches, you have locked in a profit of £850. Say it finishes at 6,200. You have a profit of £550 (110 times £5) on your up bet and of £300 (60 times £5) on your down bet. If it finishes at 6,300, you have a profit of £1,050 (210 times £5) on your up bet and a loss of £200 (40 times £5) on your down bet.

The same principle applies to individual shares as to indices. Say the spread on Acme Engineering was 100–105p and you place an up bet of £5 per share. If at the end of the betting period the price is 110p, you have made £25 (£5 times 5); if the share price is 100p, you have lost £25.

Note that you do not get the benefits of any dividend payments if you are a spread better. Nor do you get to receive annual reports or the chance to vote on any developments at the company. This is because you are not a shareholder at all, but rather a glorified gambler.

Although the potential losses from spread betting on individual shares can be large, there are ways of making the risks roughly equal to those involved in buying shares. Say you want to invest £1,000 in a company whose share price is 200p. Your maximum loss – if the company goes bust – is £1,000. So if you want to make a spread bet on the company, bet only £5 a point. Again your maximum loss is £1,000 if the share price falls to zero.

The spread betting system allows the investor to make some sophisticated gambles that would be very difficult to pull off in the conventional market. Say, for example, that you decided that shares in Vodafone were set to outperform the rest of the market. You could make an up bet on Vodafone and a down bet on the FTSE. Even if shares in Vodafone fell, you would still make money, provided that the FTSE fell more.

You could also bet that one share could outperform another: that BP would do better than fellow oil giant Shell, for example. In that case, you would place an up bet on BP and a down bet on Shell. It wouldn't matter whether the stock market soared in value or crashed during the course of your bet. Provided that BP shares did better than those of Shell, you would be in the money.

You can also use the spread betting system to protect your portfolio from a sharp fall in the market. Say you have a large portfolio of stocks which you believe will perform well over the long term, but you are worried about the possibility of a short-term crash in the UK market. You do not want to sell your shares because this will involve dealing costs or even a capital gains tax liability. The answer could be to have a down bet on the FTSE 100. If the index falls, the gains you make from the spread bet will offset the losses you make on your portfolio. And if the market rises, the gains on your portfolio will offset the loss you make on the spread bet. It's a neat trick, when it works.

And the good news is that any profits you make from spread betting will be free of capital gains or income tax. Betting duty is imposed on gambling, but that cost is absorbed within the spread charged by the bookmaker, so you will have nothing more to pay. There are also no complications such as commission or stamp duty.

Never forget, however, that spread betting is a gamble – and a potentially expensive one, at that. Many of the people who get involved tend to bet on the short-term direction of the market or of shares, and this kind of investing relies a lot more on luck than on discipline or patience. While it is possible to analyse the fundamentals behind a stock market or an individual share over the longer term, when it comes down to the next few hours or days, it can be little more than a guess. As with most forms of gambling, the odds are against you in spread betting. The bookmaker's spread is the equivalent of the zero and double zero on the roulette wheel, where the house wins.

There are a number of financial spread betting firms in operation, such as City Index, IG Index, Financial Spreads, SpreadEx and Cantor Fitzgerald. As with casino operators, they wouldn't have got into the business if they didn't expect to make a profit.

If you really fancy your ability to make money from spread betting, start by making some notional bets. Some of the firms have betting games on their websites that allow you to do this. This is a painless way to find out how quickly your gains or losses mount up.

Spread betting firms will want to check your credit references before allowing you to become a customer; after all, you could lose thousands of pounds in one gamble. If your position does move against you, they will usually ask for cash to cover your losses to date; otherwise, they will automatically close your bet.

OPTIONS

Another popular place to invest today is in the options market. An *option* gives the buyer the right, but not the obligation, to buy or sell a share at a set price within a set period of time. In return, the option buyer must pay a fee, called the *premium*. The use of the word premium is quite deliberate because, in some ways, options resemble insurance: you can use them to protect the value of your portfolio.

There are two types of option: a *call option* gives you the right to buy at a set price; and a *put option* gives you the right to sell.

Say you had a large portfolio of stocks and were worried about the potential for a sharp fall in the market. You do not want to sell your holdings because of all the dealing costs and potential capital gains tax liabilities. So you decide to place your money into the options market.

Let's say the FTSE 100 index is at 6,400, and you buy a put option on the FTSE 100 at 6,300. This is known as the *exercise price* (the price at which an option holder can buy or sell (as in this case) the shares). If the index stays above 6,300, and you do not exercise the option, then all you have lost is the premium you paid to buy the put. In this scenario, your portfolio has kept the bulk of its value; you have bought yourself some security and the money spent on the premium has not been 'wasted'. Similarly, a homeowner who has bought insurance does not mind if his house is *not* burgled or burned down.

If the index falls below 6,300, you can exercise your option. You are paid a sum in cash. This effectively offsets the loss you have suffered on the value of your portfolio and all for the cost of the premium.

Put and call options can also be used for speculative bets on the direction of prices. Say you bought a call option on Barclays' shares for £18 per share, at a time when the Barclays price was £17.50. The cost of the premium was 75p per share. If the price of Barclays jumps to £20, you exercise your right to buy at £18 per share. You then sell your shares in the market for £20 each. You have made £2 per share on a 75p investment; in other words, you have more than doubled your money. Had you simply bought Barclays shares and held on, you would have made a profit of £2.50 per share on an investment of £17.50, a return of only 14 per cent. The rewards for the right option investment are thus far more lucrative.

But beware: the percentage losses are much greater. If the price of Barclays stayed below £18.75 you would have lost money. If it stayed below £18, you would have lost all your money, whereas an investor in the underlying shares might have ended up with a small profit. The only good news is that, unlike spread betting, you know the maximum size of your loss (the premium) right from the start.

If you buy a put option when you are not insuring your portfolio, then you are gambling on the price of a share (or the index) to fall. Again, if the share price does not drop you will lose some or perhaps all of your money. But if it falls substantially, you could make a handsome profit.

Option premiums are set by supply and demand in the market. Three factors are dominant. The first is what is called the *intrinsic value* of the option. If a share price is £10 and you have a call option to buy shares at £9, then that option is obviously worth at least £1 per share. Such an option is described as being 'in the money'. A call option to buy the same share at £15 would be dubbed 'out of the money'. It would carry a much lower premium than the in-the-money option, but it is obviously worth something.

The second component of its value is time. The longer an option has before it expires, the greater its value. This is because a longer period gives the option more chance of becoming in the money. Options are normally sold at three-month intervals. So an option premium nine months out will be more expensive than an option set at the same price that expires in three months' time.

The third key factor is volatility. If the option is on a dot.com stock, whose value fluctuates 10 per cent a day, then again there is a good chance of it moving into the money. If the option is on a boring but dependable utility, it is less likely that the stock will fluctuate significantly. The premium on such options will be cheaper.

As share prices rise and fall, so does the cost of a premium. This allows an option user to make a profit without owning the shares concerned. Say a call option to buy shares at 300p (a call) carries a premium of 10p per share. If the share price rises to 400p, then the premium for a call option at 300p is clearly at least 100p. The original option buyer could then sell such an option, take the premium of 100p, and lock in a profit.

Generally, options are a vehicle best left to sophisticated investors. But if you are a novice investor who is intrigued by the way options help insure your portfolio, then you should really only buy options under the guidance of a stock-broker.

CHAPTER NINE

NEW ISSUES AND TRADING SHARES IN THE SECONDARY MARKETS

So, you have finally decided to get involved in the stock market. Perhaps this book has convinced you of the joys of share ownership. Or perhaps you were already convinced that this is the right thing for you, and simply want to know how to invest wisely. Now, what actually happens when you buy and sell shares?

There are two ways to buy shares. The first is when a company joins the market and issues its shares in a 'new issue'. The second is when you buy shares in an existing issue that are already trading on the stock market.

BUYING NEW ISSUES

When you buy shares in a new issue you normally have to do so via the stockbroker or investment bank of the company concerned. In some cases, the broker will put adverts in newspapers, inviting potential investors to apply. In other cases, you may be able to apply via the Internet. In others, your stockbroker may be able to get you shares in the issue.

Many new issues do not allow private investors to get involved. For a checklist, it is worth looking in the *Investors*

Chronicle, a weekly personal finance magazine, which lists all the forthcoming new issues. If, under the heading 'Likely method of issue', the table says 'Placing,' that means it is unlikely you will get shares. Under a placing, the investment bank or stockbroker that is handling the deal places the stock with a few selected clients. These are likely to be big institutions such as the Prudential or Standard Life. Only if the table uses the word 'Offer' will you get the chance to invest. Under an offer, shares are made available to all potential investors.

Once you've properly researched a company and decided to invest, the three most common questions you must ask yourself are:

(1) Is the price right? Companies will often suggest a potential price range – rather than a set price – at which its shares will be sold. This allows their advisers to test the likely demand. If investors are keen, the price will be set at the top of the range; if they are unenthusiastic, it will be set near the bottom. If your research indicates that the company has a good prospect for success, and the share price seems reasonable, then complete the application form and send off your cheque. In some cases, you will have to do this without knowing the exact price you will have to pay – just the range. So you must be convinced that the shares are attractive even if they are priced at the top of the range.

(2) How many shares should I apply for? All new issues will have some minimum investment amount, usually a few hundred pounds. If that is all you can afford, then the decision is easy. But if you want more shares than the minimum, things can become tricky. If the issue is popular, then demand will exceed supply, and investors like you won't get all the shares they want. Companies usually react to this in two ways. First, they limit the shares available to each private investor so that everyone gets a small but equal number.

Investors in Interactive Investor International, which floated in February 2000, received just 145 shares each, worth £217 at the flotation price. Mind you, perhaps they were lucky to get so few – by April 2001 the share price was just 21p, making 145 shares worth only £30.45. The second approach is to have a ballot. In this scenario, lucky investors will get a set amount of shares each, while the unlucky ones get nothing at all.

Your allocation of shares will generally be larger in the second method than in the first, but it still may not be as large as you want. While it may be tempting to apply for more shares than you really want in the first method – on the expectation that you will get, say, half of what you applied for – this can be a very dangerous strategy. The issue may be a failure, with investors being unwilling to buy all the shares available. If it fails, you will get all the shares you apply for, but the price will fall sharply when the shares start trading, and your losses could be substantial. And you have to pay the money up front. It could be weeks before you can sell the shares since you will have to send in a cheque well before the shares start trading on the market and it takes time for the bank to send you your share certificate. In the meantime, your cash will be earning no interest.

The good news, however, is that buying shares in a new issue does not incur stamp duty and there are no broker's commissions. If you send off a cheque for £1,000, then your £1,000 will only be used to purchase shares.

(3) What happens if my application is successful – or unsuccessful? If your application is successful, then you will be sent a certificate or other document proving entitlement to the shares. You may find, however, that this doesn't happen in time to allow you to sell on the first day the shares start trading. You should buy new issues for the long term. But if the share price doubles on the first day you may well be tempted to take some profits. A new issue that was a bargain at 100p may look expensive at 200p. Many stocks start trading on a 'when issued' basis, which allows institutions – who are certain of their share allocations – to deal, but forces private investors to wait until the paperwork is completed. This gap lasts around a week. This is undoubtedly an unfair system, but private investors should not get too upset: remember, you should be buying new issues for long-term investment, not for short-term speculation.

If your application is unsuccessful, or only partly successful (you get some, but not all, of the shares you applied for), you will get a refund cheque from the broker or investment bank behind the deal. Unfortunately, this can take weeks rather than days. If you don't receive a refund after a couple of weeks, you should contact the broker handling the issue.

BUYING AND SELLING SHARES IN THE SECONDARY MARKET

New issues represent only a very small part of the activity that goes on in the stock market. Most share trades involve established companies that were issued years ago (1 billion–2 billion shares are traded in London every day). These shares are said to trade in the secondary market.

As soon as you get involved in buying and selling established shares, you can incur up to three additional types of cost:

Stamp duty This is a government tax imposed on those who buy (not sell) shares. The rate is 0.5 per cent of the total value of the trade. (At this writing, there is much discussion about abolishing the stamp duty.)

Commission If you deal though a stockbroker, they will charge a commission for bringing buyer and seller together. (Almost all deals are done through a stockbroker, but it is possible to buy and sell from a friend without involving a broker.) Brokers normally have two levels of commission: a minimum cash amount and a percentage. For example, they could have a 1 per cent commission with a minimum of £15. Anyone dealing in a sum of under £1,500 would thus pay the minimum of £15; a deal worth £2,000 would attract commission of £20. Some brokers have sliding scales of commission for large sums.

Bid-offer spread Certain shares will only be available from so-called market makers, financial institutions who buy shares into and sell shares out of their own inventory. A market maker will buy shares from investors at the bid price and sell securities to investors at another, higher price known as the offer price or the asked price. The difference between the two prices is called the bid-offer spread, and it represents a cost to investors. The spread will be widest in smaller companies because there are fewer market makers as well as less trading activity. The spread is narrowest for stocks included in the FTSE 100. So when you decide to buy shares, remember that some of your money will be swallowed up by those costs.

If you buy £1,000 worth of shares, you will have to pay an additional £5 of stamp duty and around £15 in commission. Your total cost would therefore be £1,020. However the immediate resale value of your shares might be only £990 because of the spread. In other words, your investment starts with an immediate loss of around £30, or 3 per cent, which explains why frequent trading ('churning') is such a bad idea. The costs eat remorselessly into your returns.

PRICE-SETTING

How are prices set? In the UK, there are currently two different price-setting mechanisms: SEAQ and SETS.

The SEAQ (Stock Exchange Automated Quotation) system

now applies only to companies outside the FTSE 100 index. Under this system, the share traders known as market makers offer two-way prices (a bid price and an offer price) for individual stocks. For example, they might offer to buy Acme Construction shares from investors at 450p and sell them to investors at 460p (the 10p difference, known as the spread, represents their potential profit).

If you are buying or selling a stock that is traded under SEAQ, it will be up to your broker to get the best price available. If, for example, market maker A offered bid and offer prices of 450p–460p and market maker B's bid-offer prices are 455p–465p, a good broker should try to get the best price for his customer. If he were buying shares on behalf of a customer, he would try to buy them at the lowest offer price – 460p rather than 465p. If he were selling shares on behalf of a customer, he would try to sell them at the highest bid price – 455p, rather than 450p.

This is a reasonably open process since all market maker quotes are available on screen. But sometimes it might not run smoothly. As well as prices, market makers also quote the size of deal. This is the quantity of shares (e.g. 1,000 shares) they are prepared to trade at the quoted prices. So if you want to buy or sell a large amount of shares, it could be that the market maker may want to revise his price.

Also, some market makers may fall 'asleep at the wheel' if markets are moving fast. Their on-screen prices may not bear much relation to the actual price at which they are willing to deal.

The other problem with the market maker system is the spread between bid and offer prices, which can be quite wide, especially in small company stocks. Institutional investors have tended to resent the spread and have pushed for a more open system of trading.

That prompted the move to SETS, the Stock Exchange Trading System, in 1997. Whereas SEAQ is a quote-driven system, SETS is an order-driven system. Those who want to buy shares and those who want to sell put up the quantity they want to buy and their desired price on screen. The system then matches the buy and sell orders.

The main danger of the SETS system is the chance of a 'rogue price'. Say you put in an order to buy 100 shares in BT. The regular share price is £10 but there is a dearth of orders on the system and the nearest selling quote the system can find is £12. This may be a particular danger in the first and the last minutes of the trading day when activity is low. Because of the automatic nature of the system, your order still gets processed and you end up paying £1,200 for shares that should have cost you £1,000.

There are ways of avoiding this problem. Some stock-brokers have special deals with market makers: when they quote a price that is available on screen, they will guarantee that the customer will get that price, or better.

Another way of avoiding this problem is to set a limit on the price you will be prepared to pay. Judging that limit can be a tricky issue. To continue with the example of BT, you could set a limit of £9.90, 10p below the prevailing price. The danger is that the price may not fall below £9.90 over the course of the trading session and your order will not be processed. (You can set limits for more than twenty-four hours but there will often be a charge for this service.) Alternatively, you could set a limit slightly above the current price at, say, £10.05. Your broker is obliged to get a better price than that, if possible, but if the share price suddenly moves ahead over the next minute or so, you should still get your order filled. And you have ensured that your order is not the subject of a 'rogue trade'.

The same principle applies when you come to sell your shares. You can set a limit, a price below which you are unwilling to sell your shares. This will protect you from either a rogue trade or a sudden plunge in the share price.

Another approach that you can adopt is called 'fill or kill'. In this instance, you say you want to buy 100 shares in BT at £10 each. If the deal can be done *immediately*, at that price and for that number of shares, the broker will do (or 'fill') it; if not, the order will lapse (or be 'killed').

DOING A DEAL

(1) Find a stockbroker There is a full explanation of this in Chapter 10, but let's assume for the moment that you know which shares you want to buy (or sell) and you therefore do not need advice. In this case, you can opt for what is called an *execution-only stockbroker*. You can deal with these brokers online (over the Internet), over the telephone, or through the post. In all three cases, you will need to fill in some kind of application form so the broker can perform a credit check on you before you deal.

(2) Sign the client agreement letter Assuming your credit checks go smoothly, the broker will then send you a client agreement letter setting out the terms and conditions on which you can deal. If you are happy with the terms, sign it and send it back.

(3) The next stage may depend on the individual broker If you want to buy shares, some brokers will want you to deposit money in advance. (They should place this money in an interest-bearing account.) Others will allow you to buy shares up to a pre-set credit limit. If you want to sell shares, some may also want you to send the certificates in advance. (See section below on nominee accounts). Some brokers will allow you to sell shares and trust you to send the certificates later.

(4) Buy your shares Let's assume you are all set and you want to buy £1,000 worth of shares in British Petroleum. If you are dealing by post, then all you have to do is send off your instructions in the mail, together with your cheque. Postal brokers trade at much lower commissions than those who work over the telephone or online. But the money you save on the commission might be wiped out by the change in share price during the time it takes your instructions to get through 'snail-mail'.

If you are dealing by telephone, a bit of preparation is needed. Check out the share price of BP (or whichever share you have chosen) in the newspaper, on Ceefax or Teletext, or online if you have a computer. (There are a host of different financial news websites and your stockbroker's website will probably also have a list of financial news.) Check to see if there is any big news that day that might have changed your assessment of the shares. Assuming nothing disastrous has happened, you should now be ready to call your broker.

Sometimes you will be forced to go through 'voicemail hell' before you can speak to the right person, pressing an annoying number of buttons to get the service you want, and then listening to a tinny version of Vivaldi's *Four Seasons* for what seems like aeons. If you find you consistently face a long wait before you get through, then you should think about changing your broker. Time is money, and a long wait could cost you dearly if share prices move against you while you tap your fingers and doodle.

You will normally be required to give an account number and some other form of personal identification before you can get down to discussing the terms of the deal. Try to be as clear as possible. (This is why it helps to be prepared.) State the share that you are interested in and the amount in pounds you want to invest or receive or the number of shares you want to buy or sell. The broker will then give you an *indicative price*. This lets you know what the price is in the market but is not necessarily the final price you will get. Some brokers offer to 'hold' the price for fifteen seconds while you decide. If you don't decide quickly enough, the broker will give you a new price.

If you are happy with the price, then accept the deal. The broker should then repeat back the details of the deal and ask you some question such as 'Are you happy to go ahead?' If you say yes, then the deal is done and you are legally obliged to go through with it.

DOING A DEAL ONLINE

The invention of the Internet has made share dealing a lot easier and cheaper. It has also encouraged new investors who might have been put off by the traditional image of a stockbroker as a rather superior being. Indeed, most brokers have a website where you can check out the services they offer. Unfortunately, you can't start trading straight away, but the delay can be as little as a few hours.

First, you have to apply to become a client. That can be done online. At CSFB*direct*, for example, all you have to do is fill in your bank account details, National Insurance number and e-mail address. That will allow the company to run a credit check on you. (As with any Internet site, you need to check that your details are secure. Look for the padlock symbol that indicates that the information is protected.) Provided all is well, you should get confirmation that you have been accepted as a client within two to three hours. It should then give you a log-in ID and a password so that it can recognise you whenever you want to use its service.

The next step depends on whether you want to buy or sell

shares. If you are a buyer, then the broker will want to see the colour of your money *before* you deal. If you are a seller, it will want to see the shares transferred into its nominee account before it will trade on your behalf. In both cases, this is designed to protect the broker from loss. If it made a buy order on your behalf and you failed to pay up, it would be liable to go through with the deal. Similarly, if it made a sell order, and it turned out you did not really own the stock, it would have to go through the rigmarole and cost of obtaining the stock in order to sell it.

So if you want to buy shares you will have to wait until you can get money to your broker before you can trade. If you have a debit card, and enough money in your account, then this can be a matter of hours. If you are planning to trade actively, then you will probably want to keep a permanent balance in your account. Any decent broker should ensure that you receive a reasonable rate of interest on your cash.

If you want to sell, then you will have to send the broker your share certificates and complete Crest transfer forms (Crest is a central body that settles all Stock Exchange trades), and wait for them to be re-registered in a nominee name through the broker. This will probably take one to two working weeks. So if you are selling for a particular purpose – to fund a holiday or wedding, for example – it is wise to plan ahead.

Once those preliminaries are over with, dealing is pretty simple. You will normally need to know the short code or symbol that applies to the stock you are interested in – PON for Psion, for example. A good broker's website will enable you to look up that information.

Different brokers will use different systems. But a click on the trading or quote site should give you the current buy and sell prices for the shares. You can then enter the details of your order: the number of shares you want to sell or buy. The broker should then display the details of the order: the number of shares and the cost of the deal, including the details of its commission and stamp duty or other charges. If you are happy with the details, then you can click on an Accept icon (or something similar).

Those quotes will not be available for very long – only a matter of seconds or so. So if you dither too long the broker will not accept your trade. You will have to refresh the quote and take the risk that share prices will have moved against you in the meantime. (Of course, they could just as easily have moved in your favour.)

Remember that you need to have enough money in your account to be able to make the trade. If you do not, then the deal will not go through.

Your account at the broker will be debited within a few minutes or hours, so you should be able to see your cash balance fall on screen. Similarly you should be able to see your account rise if you sell shares. The broker should also give you a list on screen of the shares you have bought through it or hold through its nominee account.

The next stage in online dealing will be through your television set. This will only be available through digital TV services such as Open, which already allows shopping via your set. Early demonstrations indicate that TV dealing will be very like the Internet service described above. You will be able to look at share prices, the main indices, the latest financial news and some company details. You can then, using the remote control, register for the broker's service and then buy and sell shares. As with the Internet, you will need IDs and passwords to stop your nine-year-old buying 10,000 shares of Microsoft by mistake, or in mischief. TV dealing may well open up the stock market to those people who either do not have a personal computer or who find the whole business of websites, mice and portals confusing and off-putting.

AFTER THE TRADE

What happens next after the trade is done? Whether you have dealt by post, telephone or the Internet, you will be sent a contract note outlining the terms of the deal. If there are any problems with the deal, get on to your broker straight away. It may be possible to sort it out.

If you have sold shares, and you have a share certificate, you will be required to send the certificate back straight away. You will also need to fill in a Crest transfer form. The Crest form is fairly simple: you need to fill in the name of the company, the number of shares (in words and figures), your full name and then attach your signature.

If you have bought shares, and you do not have money deposited with the broker, you will need to send off a cheque. (There are alternative ways of paying: you can get your bank to transfer the money and some online brokers will let you pay with a debit card.)

Your stockbroker will send a message to Crest, giving details of the deal. The other party of the deal will do the same. Provided the details match (and payment is made), Crest will notify the registrar of the company concerned. (A registrar is simply a financial entity who keeps the details of a company's share register; this is a service often undertaken by departments of banks.) The registrar will then replace the name of the old owner of the shares with that of the new.

Once the certificate or the shares are sent off, the next event is the settlement date. Settlement is one of the more complicated subjects on the London Stock Exchange at the moment. The standard settlement date is called T+3, which means that the parties have three working days after the trade date (T) to settle the deal. This is pretty easy when institutions are involved and money can be electronically shifted from one account to another.

But T+3 is impossible to achieve for some private investor deals. By the time the private investor receives the contract note from the stockbroker at least one working day will have elapsed. Even if the client immediately sends back a cheque, it will take another working day to arrive. It then takes a further three working days to process the cheque. All that takes at least five working days.

Many stockbrokers who deal with private clients accordingly operate a T+10 system, in which it takes ten working days for the payment to go through. This allows a little more breathing space for everyone concerned. (The stockbroker will have to have a special arrangement with a market maker to operate this system.) If you do not pay within the ten days, then the broker will remind you by telephone or post. If they get no response, then they have the right to cancel the deal and you will be liable for any costs you incur. So it is wise not to do a big share deal the day before you go on holiday.

Some brokers go further and operate a T+20 or even longer system. This actually allows investors to indulge in a practice that used to be known as 'trading within the account'.

In the past all Stock Exchange trades were settled at the end of two-week periods, called accounts. This made it possible to buy shares early in the account and sell them later (or vice versa) without handing over any cash. Say you bought 1,000 shares at £1 each on the first day of the account. You would only have to pay for that deal on the Friday of the following week. If the price jumped to £1.20, you could sell the shares on, say, the following Wednesday, and make an instant profit (minus, of course, the commission costs). If the price slumped to 80p, however, you would either have to hang on in the hope of a recovery (in which case you would hand over the £1,000 at the end of the account) or sell and cut your losses. It was a great way for speculators to make short-term gambles on the market.

A similar type of deal can now be done through brokers such as T.D. Waterhouse. You can arrange to buy shares using a T+20 system, and sell them again using a T+5 or even shorter settlement. That way, you can close out the deal before you have to hand over any money.

It goes almost without saying that this useful speculative device can be highly dangerous. It is fine if you actually have the money to pay for the stock but simply want to get a 'free ride' on the market. But it would be tempting for investors to speculate with money they didn't have. If you can make an instant profit on £1,000 of shares, why not agree to buy £20,000? After all, you will never have to pay full whack. But what if the shares dipped 20 per cent? You would be £4,000 down on the deal. You would then have a stark choice: find £20,000 to buy the shares and hope that they recover, or kiss the £4,000 goodbye.

The stockbroker might find that you could not pay them at all. To guard against this situation, T.D. Waterhouse requires those who want to play the different settlement date game to pay 25 per cent of the cost of the deal upfront. This margin gives them a bit of security.

NOMINEE ACCOUNTS

Most online brokers require you to hold shares on a nominee basis, under which shares are not held in the client's name.

Traditionally, shares have been held directly, with the investor receiving a certificate to show that the shares are in his or her name. Many people like this system: it gives them a direct link with the company and a feeling of security. There can be no doubt as to the ownership of the shares. They keep the shares in a box or drawer at home.

There are drawbacks to it, however. A paper-based system is more costly to administer. Some brokers may now pass on that cost to investors in the form of a surcharge (normally around £10 per trade). Share certificates can get lost in the post, or damaged by damp or fire. If that happens you will face a charge to replace them. And while that process is taking place, you will be unable to sell shares. The third, and most significant, problem is time. A share certificate has to be sent from the owner to the broker. The broker then has to send it to the registrar, who notes the change of ownership. Then the certificate has to be sent back to the new owner. All this can take up to ten days.

As I mention above, current Stock Exchange rules maintain that share transactions are supposed to be completed in three working days. It is only because brokers have made special arrangements for delayed settlement that paper-based trades can occur at all. When the market moves to a two-day settlement period, as is expected, the gap will get even wider and the charges for paper-based trading will get even higher. As a consequence, there is a lot of pressure on investors to get rid of their share certificates.

One of the largest retail brokers in the UK, Charles Schwab, moved to nominee trading only as of June 2000. That means that all their existing clients will have had to transfer their shares into a nominee account if they wished to continue dealing with the firm.

Brokers point out that the real proof of ownership of a share is not the certificate itself, but the entry of the shareholder's name on the company's register – so certificates do not offer as much security as many investors might think.

In nominee accounts there are no share certificates, although you will get a piece of paper from your broker (or the company) saying that the shares are being held on your behalf. This saves time, as on receipt of your instructions to sell the broker can act immediately.

TYPES OF NOMINEE SYSTEMS

Nominee accounts come in different forms. The most common approach is for your stockbroker to be the nominee, but an alternative approach is to become an individual member of the Crest settlement system.

Stockbrokers operate two different kinds of nominee systems: *designated* and *pooled*. Under the designated system, each investor's holding is recorded separately on the register, using a code. Under the pooled system, all the holdings of clients under a particular broker are lumped together as one. Brokers like the pooled system much better because it is cheaper and easier to administer; the company can send out just one dividend cheque to the broker rather than several thousand.

But nominee accounts do have some disadvantages from the investor's point of view. You may have to pay an annual fee of £50 or more for using a nominee service. (Some brokers offer the service for nothing, however.) If you are an infrequent trader, that will outweigh any additional charges for dealing with share certificates.

One further problem of nominee ownership is that it locks the investor into using that particular broker. That may be bad news if, in a busy market, your broker is slow to answer a phone or provides a poor service. If you want to get your shares out of the broker's nominee account so you can start using a different broker, you will have to pay a fee.

Another problem with nominee accounts is that annual

reports and other information from the company will be sent to your broker rather than directly to you. Some companies offer perks to shareholders (discount vouchers on their services, for example) and many investors worry that they will not receive them if they opt for a nominee holding.

Much will depend on the individual broker you use. In some cases, if you want to get the annual report or go to the meeting, the broker might impose a charge for letting you do so. In other cases, this service is free, provided you let your broker know what you want; you can even take advantage of the perks. But at the time of writing some companies, including P&O and Selfridges, refuse to give nominee shareholders any perks.

Becoming a Crest member is really something that only the more active traders will find worth while. The advantage is that you have a much more direct link to the shares you own; although there is no share certificate, there is an entry on the share register with your name on it and you will receive annual reports and all other information direct from the company. The disadvantage is that you have to pay an annual fee of £10 to become a member. This is definitely not worth while if you are just starting off with £1,000 and one stock. But the system is appealing to those investors who have built up a significant portfolio. Crest direct membership grew from 1,000 in 1997 to 30,000 in early 2001.

DAY TRADING

This is an American term that has only come into use in the past five years or so. It refers to the practice of buying and selling shares within the course of the trading day, with the aim of taking advantage of short-term price movements. To date, the main home for day trading has been in the US but the practice has been catching on in the UK.

Day traders tend to be fervent believers in the practice and you will hear tales of some people who make their living, indeed make their fortunes, from the business. But the odds are stacked against you.

First of all, you bear all the costs of dealing every time you trade. Although dealing costs are cheaper than they used to be, this is like a permanent tax on your returns. Second, you are betting on short-term movements in share prices and these are not susceptible to fundamental analysis. The odds on whether a share price goes up or down over a single day are pretty close to 50–50, so you might as well spend your days gambling on the toss of a coin.

Finally, the practice can become addictive. If you win first time, you think you have the gift and then you trade even more until all your winnings have gone. If you lose first time, you take even bigger bets to regain your losses – and that road can lead to bankruptcy. Whatever individual traders may tell you, studies in the US show that the vast majority of day traders *lose* money, sometimes more than they can afford to.

CHAPTER TEN

CHOOSING A BROKER

IN the popular imagination, stockbrokers are posh operators in pin-striped suits who speak an unintelligible finan-
cialese and look down their noses at ordinary people like
you and me. One can easily imagine them sneering at our
investing naïveté, our measly income, and our general unso-
phistication about money matters. While this cliché, like most,
has a grain of truth to it – there *are* brokers who won't return
your calls unless you have boatloads of money – it wildly
overstates the general reality.

In fact, there are plenty of brokerage firms who would be
happy to answer your questions about the market, and to
work with you as long as you have a little money to invest.
And if you choose to deal over the Internet, you probably
won't need to speak to a real, live broker at all.

Many people are surprised to learn that I use a stockbroker.
The assumption is that because I am a professional financial
adviser I must know everything about every possible investment opportunity. But of course this is impossible. Having a
broker is like having a second set of eyes and ears. Actually,
I use two brokers. Both of them happen to be women, and
smart, but they have very different investment philosophies.

They each bring me suggestions about companies, sectors or markets that I might like to invest in. I am free to accept or reject any or all of their information as I see fit. After all, it is *my* money we are discussing.

There are those who have no use for a broker, but for others the broker is the second most important person in their lives (after the person they love, or have sex with). Yes, the broker relationship is *that* important. As such, I cannot over-emphasise the importance of networking your way to an honest, creative and hard-working investment adviser.

Once you have found such a person, you should talk to him (or her) and ask them questions – even 'stupid' questions – at least once a quarter. Indeed, you should be (politely) demanding what is so special about their services, and what they can do for you.

Not all brokers work in the City of London. There are brokers scattered throughout the United Kingdom, whose offices you can visit if you wish. Or you may prefer to deal with them over the telephone or the Internet. If you want a list of brokers, you can obtain a free directory from the Association of Private Client Investment Managers and Stockbrokers (APCIMS).

Before we discuss how to choose a broker, let me tell you how *not* to choose one: by responding to an unsolicited phone call. There are unscrupulous and unregulated brokers who operate, often from offshore sites, what are called *boiler rooms*. They sell shares in high-risk (sometimes non-existent) companies that usually have some 'miracle product'. They will cold-call you and say how 'lucky old you' can have these shares at a bargain price – if you only write a cheque today and send it off to them.

Of course, the real question is: If this is such a good deal, why are you letting me, a stranger, take the profits? Surely the brokers should be piling in on their own account. And if it is such a great product, then why haven't I heard of it before? Why aren't big investors like the Prudential getting involved?

The boiler-room boys will be all charm and plausibility when they call, but *don't send them any money*. Once you do, you will never see it again. You may get them on the phone, but they'll tell you it's 'too early to sell: good news is round the corner.' If you insist on selling, they'll tell you they 'didn't receive your letter'. After a while, your phone calls will not be returned or answered. Eventually, their phone service will be shut off entirely, and your sweet-talking chums will have moved on to another boiler room, with a whole new set of promises of quick cash.

When it comes to respectable stockbrokers, there are essentially three types to choose from: execution-only, advisory and discretionary. Let us look at each of these categories in turn.

EXECUTION-ONLY BROKER

An *execution-only* broker will buy and sell shares for you. And that's it. He or she will not suggest which shares to buy, or advise you on when or what to sell. Those decisions are left up to you. Indeed, the regulators do not allow an execution-only broker to offer advice. The key advantage of execution-only brokers is that they are cheap. Their commissions are much lower than those charged by other brokers, and are extremely cheap indeed if you are willing to trade via the Internet.

Some brokers, such as Charles Schwab, also offer two levels of service. One level is designed for people who trade rarely: it has no annual charge, but it does have a fairly high commission rate. The second level is designed for active investors: in return for your annual administration fee, they charge a low trading commission. For the vast majority of first-time investors it is best to opt for the former service, the one without an annual charge.

Watch also for the difference between minimum commissions and the percentage rate. If you are a small investor, buying and selling in lots of £1,000 or less, then it will be the minimum commission that will be your main concern. If you are a much larger investor dealing in lots of £3,000–£10,000 or more, then look at the percentage. It may well be that the broker with a low minimum commission is best suited to small investors but not so cost-effective when it comes to larger amounts.

Investors should also be careful about assuming that the lowest commission automatically means the best deal. What really matters is the price you end up paying (or receiving) for your shares. Say you want to buy 1,000 shares in Acme Bank. Bucketshop will do you the deal for a commission of £15, while Topnotch charges £25. Naturally you opt for Bucketshop: Why waste money? you think. But when it does the deal, Bucketshop goes straight to a friendly market maker; the price it gets is 108p. Topnotch, meanwhile, would have shopped around and got you the shares for 105p. Your total cost via Bucketshop is £1,095 (1,000 shares at 108p plus £15), while your total cost at Topnotch would have been £1,075 (1,000 shares at 105p plus £25).

Some brokers, such as the Share Centre, offer extremely cheap commission rates but only deal at set times of the day. The disadvantage is that the price you get at that set time may not be the best available during the day. But if you are dealing in very small amounts – say £200 or so of privatisation shares – then the low cost may be far more significant than any likely price fluctuation.

The problem for investors is that commissions are known

in advance, but it is much harder to tell how good a broker is at executing your order. The same principle applies with other issues of service. How good is the broker at dealing with complaints? How quick is it at answering the phone? In the autumn of 1999 many investors found they had to wait half an hour or more to get through to their brokers, who appeared to be simply overwhelmed by demand. Share prices can move a long way in half an hour, particularly in today's volatile markets, so accessibility is an important consideration.

The best way to assess these aspects of a broker's service is to network: talk to friends and acquaintances about their experiences with particular firms. If you don't know any regular investors, try reading articles on the subject in magazines such as the *Investors Chronicle*, or going online.

Nowadays, many execution-only brokers operate over the Internet. At the moment, therefore, they are only accessible to investors who have access to a personal computer (although these services will be available over a mobile phone and the television fairly soon). In many ways stockbroking is ideally suited to the Internet. Share prices move second by second and the Internet can provide investors with up-to-date information. The Internet also removes the need for costly overhead costs – such as the stockbroker's office – and helps cut commission costs. And for those who are far away from a stockbroker, or are intimidated by meeting one, the Internet can help.

There *are* risks to using an Internet broker. Some people are uncomfortable about putting their personal financial details into a website. Before you divulge such information, check out the background of the firm. Is it registered with the Financial Services Authority? Have any of your friends dealt with it? Has it received any comment (favourable or unfavourable) in the financial press? Finally, make sure it uses the padlock symbol on its website, which indicates that your information is properly encrypted.

A decent Internet broker will offer you more than just low commissions. Its website should link you to a news service that provides breaking financial news. It should provide charts depicting the recent performance of share prices. And it should give you the option of checking the details of your portfolio online. You may be able to do all of this with a regular broker, but it will have to be done at their convenience and it will take much longer.

Before you choose an online broker, it is worth checking out some of the sites on the web that provide information about the industry. The *Investors Chronicle* recommends three sites:

- *www.fool.co.uk/brokers/brokers.htm*
- *www.iii.co.uk/ukonlinetrading/*
- *www.moneyworld.co.uk/trading/*

As with other execution-only brokers, it is natural to look at commission costs as the main factor that differentiates these sites. But there are lots of other factors to consider as well. Does the broker charge an administration fee for keeping your shares in nominee form, or for handling dividends? What sort of interest rate does it pay on cash held in the account? Will it accept limit orders and other variations? What type of securities does it cover (international shares, options etc.)? Does it give access to broker research?

The moneyworld site (address above) has a useful table that sets out both the charges for share trades of different sizes, and any administration charges imposed by the broker. The Motley Fool site (address above) lists the details of the individual broker services, such as dealing limits and the ability to trade in overseas shares.

It is worth taking time choosing an *execution-only broker*, especially if they want you to use a nominee service. This service (fully explained in Chapter 9) saves time and paperwork when dealing. But it means your shares are in the broker's name, not yours, and that can be a real pain if the broker's service is unsatisfactory. If you want to switch brokers, you could face considerable time and expense trying to extricate yourself.

ADVISORY BROKER

An *advisory broker* gives you more help than the execution-only broker. As the name suggests, you can get advice from the broker on which shares to buy or sell. This service falls into two types.

In the standard advisory service, you take the initiative. Say you want to buy shares in Tesco. You ring up the broker and ask what they think of Tesco shares. They will refer either to their research department's report on the stock, or to the general pool of research produced by other, bigger brokers. If they agree that the share is worth buying, you will purchase the shares through them. Because you have received advice, you will have to pay a commission level higher than you would pay for using an execution-only broker.

The second category of service, called *advisory portfolio dealing*, puts more control in the hands of the broker. The broker looks after your shares, which will normally be held in a nominee account, and rings you whenever they think a share should be bought or sold. That gives you a right of veto over changes in your portfolio without the need to spend all day monitoring the stock market.

It can be tough deciding whether an advisory broker offers the best service for you. Asking friends who have used the service is an obvious guide. Another is to check out the company's website on the Internet, which may give an indication of the quality of its research. You should also find out whether you will be allocated a named broker to deal with. If so, you need to feel comfortable with and confident about that person. Do they appear to pressure you into buying or selling shares (they may be after the maximum commission), or do they give the impression of having your best interests at heart? It's also important that the broker will answer the phone when you need them. It will be highly annoying (and stressful) if you find that, when the going gets tough, your broker goes AWOL.

DISCRETIONARY BROKER

A *discretionary broker* is someone who takes charge of your entire portfolio. They make all the decisions for you about which shares to invest in and when to sell them. In a way, this is rather like investing in a unit or investment trust. You hand over your money to a manager and rely on them to invest the money wisely. But this is a far more personalised portfolio than a trust would provide. The broker will tailor your portfolio based on whether you want income or growth, what level of risk you are prepared to bear, and so on. A discretionary broker should also handle much of the financial detail work: your dividend payments, capital gains tax planning, and so on. The idea is that you need hardly give your investment a moment's thought.

This can be an ideal service for those who are too busy to watch over their investments, or simply lack the patience, confidence or enthusiasm to do so. The snag is that discretionary brokerage services aren't available to everybody, and aren't cheap.

Indeed, discretionary services are usually only available to the very wealthy – those with a portfolio of some £100,000, or more. Such brokers are often used by 'old money' people (those with inherited wealth), or by those who have suddenly become cash-rich by virtue of selling their business. There are more of these people than you might think. Research indicates that in the UK there are about 1.3 million people with £100,000 or more of assets to invest. Not surprisingly, this bunch is highly sought after by the big financial groups.

PRIVATE BANKERS

Close relations of the discretionary brokers are the private bankers. These folk also offer to look after all your financial needs, including the handling of your bank account, credit cards and the like. The private banks may be a division of a big clearing bank, such as Lloyds TSB. They may be overseas banks – the Swiss banks are famous for providing this kind of service. Or they may be small specialists, such as Coutts or Leopold Joseph. Some companies, notably the big US investment banks, offer private banking services, but these tend to be restricted to the very wealthy: those with over $5 million (£3.5 million).

Some investors will undoubtedly want the de luxe service provided by private bankers. But watch out for the cost. How much are you paying in fees? Unless your finances are particularly complicated, you can probably get professional fund management elsewhere cheaper, by buying shares in an international investment trust, for example, or units in an index-tracker fund.

Watch out also for the practice of 'churning'. This occurs when a broker handling your account makes an excessive number of trades in a year. They may claim they are simply switching your portfolio to take advantage of market opportunities, but every time they trade their firm earns a commission – which comes out of your pocket.

On a similar point, don't be impressed by marble halls and oak-panelled walls covered with Old Masters. Who paid for all that luxury? Previous clients. There is an old Wall Street joke about the naïve young stockbroker who is taken to the harbour to gaze upon the partners' fabulous yachts. 'And where,' asked the ingénu, 'are the customers' yachts?' Any fool can spend other people's money; what you need is someone who can earn you enough to pay for your own yacht.

You are the customer; the broker is the service provider. Many English people seem to forget this equation, or are too cowed to enforce it. To help you over this hurdle, here are a few practical tips on choosing an investment adviser.

A broker or private banker can claim investment expertise until they're blue in the face, but unless they can produce hard data to back it up don't believe them. Insist on seeing performance statistics. If the broker replies that 'each client is unique,' and that it is impossible to give an overall picture, ask to see some kind of pooled or model portfolio that will give an indication of their performance.

Before you choose any stockbroker, make sure they are legitimate. The regulation of stockbrokers has just been revamped. A new body called the Financial Services Authority (FSA) has taken over the powers of the Securities and Futures Authority (SFA) and the Investment Management Regulatory Organisation (IMRO). The FSA is designed to be a sort of super-regulator that oversees all aspects of the financial services industry.

All brokers will have to be authorised by the FSA. To check whether this is the case, you can call the body's central register on 0845 606 1234 or look up a firm on its website, at *www.fsa.gov.uk*.

If you want to complain about your broker, you first have to pursue the complaint through the company's internal procedures. If that doesn't give you satisfaction, the next step is to write to the Financial Ombudsman. At the time of writing, the Financial Ombudsman was about to take over from eight separate predecessors who covered different sectors of the financial services industry. The Ombudsman will listen to both sides of a dispute, and decide whether you have been badly treated. There is no guarantee he will find in your favour. If he does, you will be entitled to compensation, although it is not yet clear how much that will be.

If the firm handling your shares goes bust, there is a Financial Services Compensation Scheme set up by the government. The details are still being sorted out, but under the old scheme investors were entitled to compensation up to a maximum of £48,000.

In the case of fraud, brokers should have insurance to cover any potential problems, including computer fraud. This is another point to ask about when you contact a broker.

GLOSSARY

Accumulation unit Type of unit in a trust where the income is rolled up within the price rather than paid out to investors.

Advisory broker A broker who, in return for a higher commission rate, offers advice to clients on their share-dealing decisions.

Advisory portfolio dealing Service provided by an advisory broker in which the broker initiates decisions but the client has the right of veto.

Alternative Investment Market Forum where young companies are traded on the London Stock Exchange.

Annual charge Fee charged by a fund manager every year, based on a percentage of the value of the trust. For a unit trust it is normally 1 or 1.5 per cent. Some investment trusts charge less than 1 per cent.

Annual general meeting (AGM) The main meeting held by a company every year, at which the company reports on its progress, appoints new directors and conducts other routine business.

Bar chart Chart which shows the range of a share price's daily movement as a vertical line with the closing price marked as a horizontal tick against that line.

Bid price Price received by investors when they sell units.

Bid-offer spread 1) The difference between the price at which a market maker will buy shares from an investor (the bid price) and the price at which a market maker will sell shares to an investor (the offer or asked price). The bid is always lower than the other, and is therefore a profit for the market maker. 2) Difference between bid and offer prices in a conventional unit trust that reflects the initial charge and some dealing costs.

CAC 40 Leading stock market indicator in France, comprising forty shares.

Call option The right, but not the obligation, to buy a fixed amount of shares (compare *put option*) at a set price before the end of a set period.

Capital share One type of share in a split capital trust. It pays no income but benefits from most, or all, of the trust's growth. (See *split capital trust*.)

Constant ratio plan Approach to investing that involves keeping a set proportion of the money you have invested in different types of assets.

Contract note Statement you receive from a stockbroker, if you have bought or sold shares, or from a unit trust manager if you have bought or sold units that shows the terms of the deal.

Convertible preference share Share that offers a fixed dividend but also the opportunity to switch into an ordinary share.

Crest Official body that settles share trades, matching the instructions sent by buyers and sellers.

DAX Leading stock market indicator in Germany, comprising thirty shares.

Day trading Practice of buying and selling shares within the course of a day, with the hope of taking advantage of short-term price movements.

Debt security An investment instrument, such as a bond or gilt, through which you lend an issuer your money. In return, the issuer agrees to pay you interest at regular intervals and agrees to repay the principal or face value of the loan on a fixed date, called the maturity date.

Designated nominee System for holding shares without certificates but with an indication on the register of the name of the underlying holder.

Discount Amount by which the share price of an investment trust is lower than net asset value per share (see *net asset value*). Alternatively, a reduced charge or price.

Discretionary broker A full service broker who takes complete charge of your portfolio, making all the investment decisions.

Distribution units Type of unit where income is paid to investors.

Dividend That portion of a company's earnings that its Board of Directors decides to pay out to its shareholders. Not all companies pay a dividend but most do so – at least twice a year.

Dividend yield The net annual dividend of a share divided by the share price and expressed as a percentage.

Double bottom Pattern of two successive lows in market movements, at roughly the same level so the chart makes a formation in the shape of a w. Seen as a bullish sign.

Double top Pattern of two successive highs in market

movements, each at roughly the same level, so the chart makes a formation in the sign of an m. Seen as a bearish sign.

Dow Jones Industrial Average Best-known US stock market indicator, comprising thirty prominent companies.

Earnings per share The profits of a company (after deductions such as operating expenses, interest and tax) divided by the number of shares in issue.

Earnings yield Earnings per share divided by the share price and expressed as a percentage. The inverse of the P/E ratio.

Elliott waves Pattern of market movements in which an up phase (consisting of three up and two down waves) is followed by a down phase (two down and one up waves).

Equity security Also called a share. An investment instrument representing part-ownership in a business enterprise and giving its holder the right to receive dividends. Ordinary shares and preference shares are both equity securities.

Execution-only broker Broker who offers cheap dealing services, usually over the telephone or over the Internet, with no advice.

Exercise price The fixed price at which an option holder could buy shares (under a call option) or sell (under a put option) a fixed amount of stock.

Extraordinary general meeting (EGM) Special meeting held by companies to allow investors to vote on unusual events, such as big acquisitions.

Fibonacci numbers Set of numbers used by some chartists in which each successive number is the sum of the two preceding numbers.

Financial Ombudsman Body that arbitrates in complaints between individuals and financial companies.

Financial Services Authority Government body that regulates the financial services industry.

Forward price Method of unit trust pricing under which the price you deal is calculated at the end of the current trading day, based on that day's closing share prices.

Gearing Borrowing undertaken by an investment trust to try to enhance returns to investors. Alternatively, a measure of the level of debt taken on by a company relative to the value of its share capital or assets.

Head-and-shoulders Pattern of three successive peaks in market movements of which the second is the highest. Seen as a sign of an imminent price reversal.

Historic price Method of unit trust pricing under which the price at which you deal is calculated on the previous trading day's closing share prices.

In the money An option where the exercise price is lower than the market price (in the case of a call) or higher than the market price (in the case of a put).

Income share One class of share in a split capital investment trust which offers a high level of income but may result in no capital gain or even a loss.

Income unit Same as distribution unit (see above).

Index-tracker (See *tracker fund*.)

Individual Savings Accounts A tax-advantaged account in which investors can own cash, shares, unit or investment trusts, or insurance. They will pay no capital gains tax on their profits and will get a modest tax break on any income.

Initial charge Fee charged by a manager when investors first put money into a unit trust or OEIC. Normally around 5 per cent.

Intangible assets Something owned by a company that does

not have a physical form, such as copyright or a brand name, but which still has lots of value.

Investment bank Financial company that earns fees in return for advising companies on share and bond issues and on takeovers. Many investment banks also have extensive share and bond trading arms and fund-management subsidiaries.

Line chart Standard graph format, with a price movement shown as a solid line.

Liquidity The ease with which an asset can be bought and sold, or turned into cash. Shares in a big company, such as BP, are very liquid; it is easy to find a buyer within seconds. But one might go days or weeks without finding a buyer for shares in an unquoted company.

Market capitalisation The total stock market value of a company, calculated by multiplying the number of shares in issue by the current share price.

Market maker A financial institution that stands ready each trading day to buy securities into and sell securities out of its own inventory.

Market value The price investors are willing to pay for a share, or a company, in the market.

Moving average Technical tool that uses the average closing level over a set number of days. Once a new closing level is recorded, the first of the series drops off.

NASDAQ (acronym for National Association of Securities Dealers Automated Quotation System) US electronic stock market in which many of the world's best-known technology stocks are traded.

Net asset value 1) The value of a company's assets after the value of all its debts has been deducted. 2) For a unit or investment trust, the market value of the securities in the trust's portfolio minus all on-going expenses such as management fees.

Nikkei 225 Leading stock market indicator in Japan.

Nominee account System for holding shares without certificates.

OEIC Short for open-ended investment company. Similar to a unit trust but with a simpler structure. There is only one price and any charges are added on top.

Offer price Price paid by investors when they buy units or in some cases shares.

Online broker Stockbroker who allows you to buy or sell over the Internet.

Option Financial contract that gives the buyer the right, but not the obligation, to buy, or sell, a fixed quantity of shares at a set price before the end of a set period. (See *exercise price*.)

Ordinary share The most common type of share. It represents part-ownership of the assets and profits of a business. Each ordinary share has the right to vote on important company decisions and to receive dividends.

Out of the money An option where the exercise price is higher than the market price (in the case of a call) or lower than the market price (in the case of a put). (Compare *In the money*.)

Par value The nominal value of a share, created for legal reasons. It has no relation to the market price.

PEG ratio The price-earnings ratio of a share divided by the trend rate of annual earnings growth.

Penny stock A share with a very low price, normally under £1.

Placings Method by which new shares are sold. They are

placed with institutional investors, rather than offered to the general public.

Point-and-figure chart Chart that shows successive changes in the direction of prices as a series of Xs (for upward movement) and Os (for downward movement).

Pooled nominee System for holding shares without certificates where the holdings are lumped together under one name, usually that of the stockbroker.

Pound-cost averaging An investment or savings scheme where a person invests a fixed amount of money at regular intervals (e.g. monthly) in a unit trust. This money buys fewer units when the price is high, more when it is low. This lowers the average cost of a unit.

Preference share Type of share that pays a fixed dividend and gives its holder preference over ordinary shareholders in receiving dividends and making claims on the company's assets in a liquidation.

Premium Amount by which the share price of the investment trust is greater than the net asset value per share (see *net asset value*). Also the fee paid by an investor who buys an option contract. (See *option*.)

Price per user Ratio used to value Internet stocks. Relates the market value of the company to the total number of users of the service or website.

Price-earnings ratio The share price of a company divided by the earnings per share.

Price-to-cash flow ratio The share price of a company divided by the cash earnings per share.

Price-to-sales ratio Either the total value of a company divided by its total sales or the share price divided by its sales per share.

Prospective dividend yield Dividend yield calculation that uses forecast, rather than announced, dividend payments. (See *dividend yield*.)

Prospective price-earnings ratio P/E calculation that uses forecast, rather than announced, earnings per share.

Prospectus Document issued at the time of a new issue, giving details of the finances of the company, the background of the directors etc.

Put option The right, but not the obligation, to sell a fixed quantity of shares at a set price before the end of a set period. (Compare *Call option*.)

Registrar Person or company who records the changes of ownership in a company's shares.

Resistance level Term used in technical analysis, indicating a price level which the share seems unable to surpass.

Rights issue Method by which quoted companies raise additional money. Existing shareholders have first claim (rights) over the new shares.

Scrip issue Additional issue of shares which raises no new money for the company. The effect is to increase the number of shares in issue but lower the share price, leaving the overall value of the investor's holding unchanged.

Security An investment instrument that 1) represents part-ownership in a business enterprise (equity sharing), giving its holder the right to receive dividends and/or participate in the company's growth, 2) represents a loan to the issuer (debt security), for which the issuer promises to pay interest and, at regular intervals, repay the principal or face value of the loan on a set maturity date.

Settlement date The date by which money has to be paid over in respect of a share trade.

Split Capital Trust Specialised investment trust with different types of shares. (See *Capital shares*, *Income shares* and *Zero dividend preference share*.)

Spread betting A form of gambling where the gambler has to estimate whether a number, such as the goals scored in a cup final or the level of a stock market index, will be above or below a range (the spread).

Stamp duty Tax imposed by the government on share purchases.

Stock split Similar to a scrip. The issuance of additional shares to existing stockholders at no additional cost. As a result, the price of the shares drops, making them more attractive to a broad group of investors.

Stockbroker Financial company that matches buyers and sellers on the stock market in return for a commission. Stockbrokers also give advice to companies and have teams of analysts who recommend shares to investors.

Support level Term used in technical analysis, indicating a price level which the share seems unable to fall below.

T+ – Shorthand term for the settlement period. The 'T' stands for transaction or trade date. If the agreed settlement period is T+3, then money must be paid within three working days of the transaction date.

Tangible assets A company's physical assets, such as buildings and machines.

Tax credit Entry on a dividend or trust statement which shows the tax you are deemed to have paid. Basic-rate taxpayers face no further charge.

Techmark Section of the London Stock Exchange dealing with technology companies.

Tracker Fund A unit trust or OEIC that tries to match the

performance of a specific index, such as the FTSE 100 index or the FTSE All Share index. Charges are much lower than on a managed unit trust or OEIC.

Venture capitalists Professional investors who put money into high-risk projects, particularly small companies that have yet to get a stock market quote.

Warrant Security which gives investors the right to buy more shares at a set price for a fixed period of time.

Zero dividend preference share Another type of share in a split capital trust. This pays no dividends but promises a set rate of capital growth and has first claim on a trust's assets.

KNOW WHEN TO LIGHTEN UP

I debated entitling this epilogue 'Always have an exit strategy,' but I realised that this suggested trying to time the market or pick a market top – two things I don't believe are possible. However, I do think that when you buy any security (stock, bond, unit trust or investment trust) you should have an idea about how much you are willing to see the market price decline below your purchase price, before you cut your losses.

What do you do, however, when a company stock that you own has had a good run up in price? This is a trickier matter because dreams of riches start to cloud your decisions. You should begin thinking about rebalancing your portfolio or realising some of your profits. What do I mean by a good run up? That varies with the individual share. In some more stable blue chips, a 25% rise could represent a substantial gain. In some growth stocks, a 100% or 200% increase could qualify. A useful way to make this judgement is to calculate the percentage that the value of each company occupies in your total portfolio, before and after the run up. When one or more shares start to distort the overall balance, it could be time to lighten up on the shares and rebalance your portfolio.

As I have said throughout this book, having a well-diversified portfolio lessens the risk associated with having too many eggs invested in one stock or one sector. That is most assuredly the lesson that all investors should have learned from the stock market over the last two years. Many of us who bought technology stocks in the 1990s saw them double, triple, and quadruple in price. As the value of the shares rose, how many of us failed to notice that the percentage invested in each company had become overly concentrated? Very few, I suspect. Instead we focused only on the gross profits.

A prudent approach is to periodically rebalance the percentage of your money invested in each stock. Sell a portion of the securities in which you have these spectacular gains and then invest money in other shares that are not in the same sector – possibly putting the money into conservative stocks in different sectors, or even holding it as cash. Whatever you do, don't put the money back in the same sector.

Many of us resist rebalancing. We dread the pain of paying tax on a capital gain. And the anticipation of the pain leads us to make some irrational investment decisions. We hold on to the shares and come up with elaborate justifications – the most common being how low our cost basis is. As investors we should be happy to pay capital gains tax because it means we have made money. Our investment could just as easily have resulted in a loss. And to tell the truth: would you rather have a loss and pay no taxes, or have a gain on which you pay taxes? I know which choice I would make! 60% of a gain is far better than nothing!

Whatever approach you take to investing in the stock market, it is always good to keep a healthy perspective on the whole process. There are so many forces in the stock market that are beyond your individual control. The only thing you can really try to control is yourself. Don't let investing become something that defines or consumes you. I will be among the first to admit that it is gratifying (even addictive for some) to watch your net worth increase, and it is nerve-racking to watch your hard-earned money decline in value. Expect to experience wild swings between these emotions as you invest wisely – and sometimes badly. The main lesson of surviving and prospering in the stock market is this: during the good times, know when to diversify and lighten up on some of the shares you own, and during the bad times, know when to lighten up on yourself.

INDEX

Page numbers in bold indicate Glossary definitions
Page numbers in italics indicate figures